THE POSITIVE THINKING WORKBOOK

THE
POSITIVE THINKING
WORKBOOK

QUIET YOUR INNER CRITIC AND BUILD A STRONG FOUNDATION FOR A POSITIVE MINDSET

ALEXA BRAND, MS, LMFT

**ROCKRIDGE
PRESS**

For general information on our other products and services or to obtain technical support, please contact our Customer Care Department within the United States at (866) 744-2665, or outside the United States at (510) 253-0500.

Rockridge Press publishes its books in a variety of electronic and print formats. Some content that appears in print may not be available in electronic books, and vice versa.

Interior and Cover Designer: Eric Pratt
Art Producer: Samantha Ulban
Editor: Jed Bickman
Production Editor: Andrew Yackira
Production Manager: Holly Haydash

All images used under license Shutterstock.

ISBN: Print 978-1-64876-827-9
eBook 978-1-64876-249-9
R0

THIS WORKBOOK BELONGS TO:

_____

CONTENTS

INTRODUCTION viii

CHAPTER ONE
POSITIVE THINKING 101 3

CHAPTER TWO
PREPARE TO SHIFT YOUR MINDSET 15

CHAPTER THREE
CHECK IN WITH YOURSELF 29

CHAPTER FOUR
SOOTHE YOUR INNER CRITIC 55

CHAPTER FIVE
SHIFT YOUR MINDSET 79

CHAPTER SIX
EMBRACE GRATITUDE 103

CHAPTER SEVEN
BUILD YOUR SUPPORT SQUAD 129

CHAPTER EIGHT
THINK POSITIVELY EVERY DAY 153

CONCLUSION 185

RESOURCES 186

REFERENCES 187

INDEX 191

Introduction

I'm Alexa, and I've created this workbook for you. Positive thinking radically shifted my life and it will shift yours, too.

As a child, I didn't know who I was or who I wanted to be. I lived for other people. I didn't know my own voice. I felt lost, scared, and unworthy, and I was afraid to embrace my inner power. Honestly, I don't think I even knew I had power within. I just knew that I wanted to help others.

As I grew older, these feelings and patterns continued to show up in my life and only became worse. I thought that, to find happiness, I needed to change my appearance so I could garner the attention of a romantic partner. In college, I entered into emotionally abusive relationships in which I was belittled, degraded, and dehumanized. I was sexually assaulted and developed an eating disorder. The traumas of life seemed to relentlessly bring me down. Then came debilitating anxiety and depression. I could barely get out of bed; all I wanted to do was sleep so I didn't have to feel.

And I blamed myself. I thought I was weak. I felt at fault for all parts of my experience. But I also recognized that something was seriously wrong in my internal world. I knew I needed help. That's when I started to go to therapy.

In therapy, I learned the profound impacts that family patterns, societal norms, and traumatic events have had on my inner world. I realized that I had been unconsciously conditioned to reject my inner power and to give all my energy away to others. Most important, I learned and embraced the tools of positive thinking. And my entire world changed.

Day by day, I practiced positive thinking. Little by little, I began to reclaim my power and shift my inner world. There were times when I wanted to give up and times when I felt like a failure, but I persisted.

Small steps led to big changes, and the impact has been profound. I found my inner voice. I began sharing my opinions. I lived more authentically. My anxiety and depression decreased significantly. I came out as bisexual. I found a kind, loving partner to whom I am now married.

I became a therapist so that I could share these life-changing skills with others. I've worked in nonprofits, schools, and community clinics, specializing in working with diverse communities and those who have experienced trauma, including intimate partner violence and sexual assault. I've worked as an adjunct instructor for a graduate psychology program that trains therapists, and I even started my own business, Soul Compassion (SoulCompassion.com), to provide mindfulness mentorship to people looking to bring more self-compassion and mindfulness into their lives. And now I am writing this book.

I am the most aligned I've ever been in my life. Just five years ago, I would have laughed if you told me that I'd be where I am today, but here I am. That's the power of positive thinking. That's why I am sharing these transformative tools with you.

Positive thinking decreases stress, anxiety, depression, and other distressing emotions; it also increases motivation, life satisfaction, physical health, and relationship satisfaction. The benefits work their way into every aspect of your life.

In this workbook, you'll dive into positive thinking, learn more about its amazing benefits, and gain all the foundational information you need to start building a positive mindset. Furthermore, you'll find a plentiful array of prompts, exercises, practices, quotes, and affirmations to aid you on your journey.

While this book can help you make significant changes to your mindset, know that it is not a substitute for therapy, medication, or medical treatment. If you find your emotions to be debilitating to your everyday life, I encourage you to reach out for support from a mental health professional. Please know that there is no shame in getting this extra support.

Many people who see where I am at now tell me that I must have some amazing superpowers to be where I am today. But the truth is, it took time, patience, and my willingness to invest in myself. I am still actively on this journey. I encourage you to jump in—not for anyone else, but for yourself.

Know that there is so much hope for you. Everything you need for positive thinking is right there inside of you. Get ready to let it shine!

♡ Alexa

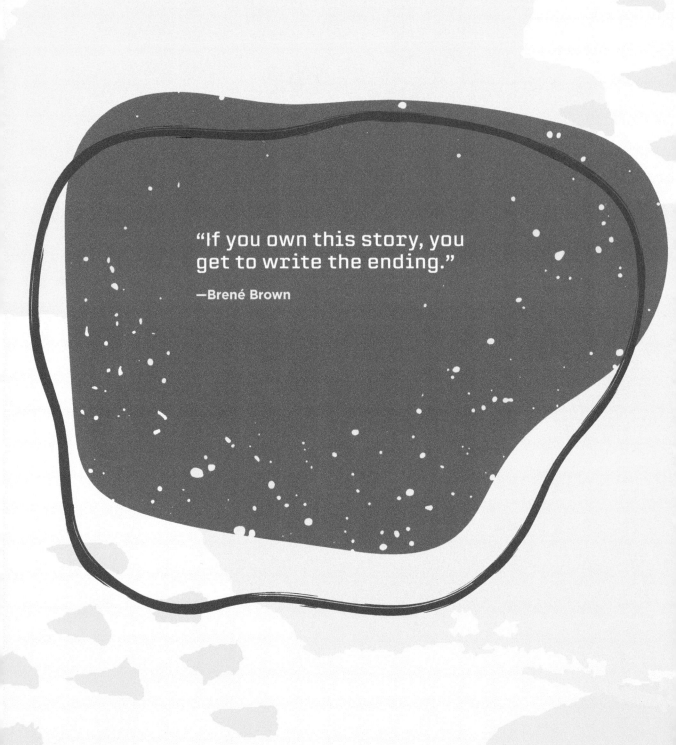

"If you own this story, you get to write the ending."

—Brené Brown

LET'S TALK ABOUT POSITIVE THINKING

When you see the words *positive thinking*, what is your immediate reaction? Do you associate them with some distant concept that's impossible to achieve? Do the words *positive thinking* make you feel self-critical and incapable? Or do they make you feel excited and hopeful?

Well, the awesome truth is that you've already taken your first step toward positive thinking by simply jumping into this book! You've shown up for yourself and set yourself up for success. In part 1, you'll learn all the foundations of positive thinking: what positive thinking means, what it doesn't mean, and how to put it into practice. You'll also learn about the profound life-changing benefits that result from the practice. I'm so excited to guide you through this beautiful journey.

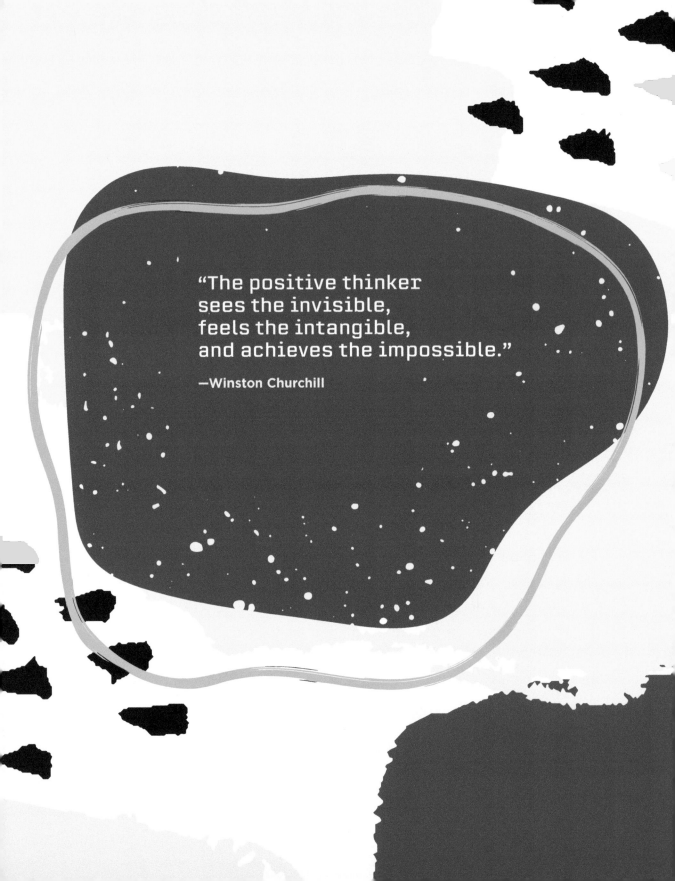

"The positive thinker
sees the invisible,
feels the intangible,
and achieves the impossible."

—Winston Churchill

CHAPTER ONE

POSITIVE THINKING 101

Positive thinking may seem like a cryptic concept, and there are many misconceptions about it, so the first thing we need to do is clearly define it. By the end of this chapter, you'll know what positive thinking is and what it isn't, and you'll understand its transformative powers. You'll also find out about the potential challenges that may arise through this journey and learn why it's been a challenge for you to have a positive mindset up to this point in time. Let's dive in!

What Is Positive Thinking?

Positive thinking is a mental tool we can use to shift from a negative, harmful mindset to a more positive, self-compassionate one. Positive thinking fosters hope and optimism by offering understanding, kindness, and acknowledgment of our incredible resilience. Research shows that we can literally rewire our brains through conscious awareness, consistent mindful practices, and patience. Believe me, even though it can take time, the benefits of shifting your mindset are so worth it!

Positive thinking involves active management of how your brain works. We break down the complex workings of your mind into units called *cognitions*, which are mental actions and processes that you engage in all the time, every day. Of course, there are endless types of cognitions as complex as the brain itself, but to train yourself into positive thinking, you need to focus on these three different types:

1. **Self-talk** is the way you talk to yourself in your head. Your self-talk can change your mood in an instant. It can motivate you or paralyze you. It can radically shift your experience of life. The goal is to bring gentle awareness to your self-talk and then transition toward kindness and understanding (aka self-compassion). This transformative experience increases the positivity of your mindset.

2. **Perceptions** are the views and interpretations that you hold of the world. These perceptions can be about anyone or anything, such as you, other people, material objects, specific topics, concepts, places, etc. When you start to embrace a more comprehensive, thoughtful approach to your perceptions, you can open your mind to positive perspectives that bring significant healing. This means moving away from "all-or-nothing" thinking patterns and rigid, inflexible understandings of the world. It also means understanding where your perceptions originally came from (e.g., family, society, media).

3. **Narratives** are the long-term stories your mind tells about you and the world around you. These narratives play a huge role in how you interact with the world. They're originally thrust upon us by external sources starting at birth and become stronger over time as they are nourished by our internal self-talk and perceptions. Negative narratives limit you to rigid, hopeless thinking and reinforce harmful behaviors. Just like with perceptions, it's important to know where your narratives came from. Shifting your narratives with empathy will foster greater truth and mental peace.

In general, we tend to perceive our thoughts as facts. In reality, they aren't. As humans, we're limited in our understanding of the universe. Therefore, we certainly shouldn't believe everything we think. Understanding this human limitation in itself can help us shift to a more positive mindset. Your thoughts are just thoughts. Nothing more. Nothing less. Once you can give less weight to your thoughts and engage in them with more self-compassion, you will foster increased tranquility and wellness.

What Positive Thinking Isn't

Positive thinking is not viewing everything in a positive light or pretending everything is okay when it's not. That would be toxic positivity. Toxic positivity is the assumption that we have to maintain "positive vibes" even in times of great suffering. It assumes you should ignore your suffering, which is actually a harmful practice in itself. When you ignore your suffering, you are not allowing yourself to process your emotions, and they become buried inside of you. This only intensifies your suffering.

Additionally, there is no such thing as being perfect at positive thinking. We are human. We are all learning, growing, healing, and adapting to new situations. We need to be flexible when embracing positive thinking, which means there may be times when things don't work out quite as we expected.

Finally, positive thinking is not selfish. When you're able to focus on your own well-being, you become better set up to help others in more abundant ways. As the adage goes, "You can't pour from an empty cup."

Why Do We Struggle to Think Positively?

It's human nature to fixate on the negative and ignore the positive. Why? Evolution. For more than 90 percent of our existence, we human beings lived as hunter-gatherers and our brains evolved to support that lifestyle. As time has passed, however, technology has advanced at a much faster pace than our brains can keep up with.

Prior to technological advances, humans needed to be constantly vigilant about their surroundings to survive. Large, dangerous threats like wild animals were a constant risk. Therefore, human brains were wired to quickly activate the fight-or-flight response (the emergency alert response of our brains) so that we could defend ourselves, run away, or play dead. The problem is that our brains still engage in this distressing response even though we no longer face these same types of threats on a regular basis.

Negative thinking also makes us feel as though we have some sense of control. Have you ever told yourself, "If only I had done x, y, or z, then I wouldn't have experienced that horrible situation"? It can be awful to feel out of control, and questioning our actions makes us feel like we could have controlled the outcome. We engage in self-critical, past-fixated, and future-focused thinking patterns with the goal of preventing distressing experiences and to try to protect ourselves. We are concerned that if we aren't constantly hypervigilant, then we won't be able to prevent the next bad thing. There's nothing wrong with healthy awareness and safety preparation, but when we hyper-fixate on what's gone wrong and embrace self-criticism, we begin to sink into a negative mindset.

Furthermore, most of us are not ever taught how to think in a positive way. Western individualistic society tends to oppress positive thinking by normalizing self-criticism, and the majority of us did not receive any emotional education as children. Family and/or social norms have made us internalize pervasive messages of shame. We begin to believe that we need to be hard on ourselves to be successful, to achieve our dreams, and to live the "perfect life."

Due to these constant messages that begin at birth, these shame pathways in our brains are quite strong. People who are marginalized (e.g., women, BIPOC, LGBTQ+ people, disabled folx, and low SES) are presented with even greater oppression, which leads to more intensified internalized shame for these people. Whether we choose to or not, we are constantly internalizing these messages.

So now that you've learned why it's a struggle to think positively, notice if you can offer yourself a statement of more understanding and kindness, such as "Wow, it makes sense why I haven't been able to cultivate positive thinking in my life." Cut yourself some slack! We were set up for failure in so many ways. Now you are aware, and awareness is the first step toward change.

THE NEGATIVE BIAS TRAP

You are hardwired to fixate on the negative. Your brain's biological nature is to attune to negative stimuli and then ruminate on this negativity, which then sets you up to make decisions based on negativity. This is the negative bias trap. The evolutionary purpose of this trap is to protect you from harm. The downside of it is that you probably don't feel too great when trying to manage everything life brings your way. This biological hardwiring is why it takes the active, consistent awareness and practice of positive thinking to overcome this negative bias trap. But the good news is that you can shift this way of thinking, overcome your biological tendencies, and rewire your brain to be more positive. Take a moment of gratitude for both your brain's protection and flexibility!

Where Do You Struggle with a Positive Mindset?

Your struggle with a positive mindset can show up in many different areas of your life, including your romantic relationships, your family relationships, your friendships, your relationship with yourself, your career and finances, your creative outlets, your health and fitness, your body image, your relationship with food, your goal work, and even your relationship with time. The list truly goes on and on. Perhaps there are only a few areas in which you struggle to think positively, or perhaps you struggle with positive thinking in all areas of your life. Know that, either way, there is significant hope for you. By applying the tools in this workbook, you'll begin to improve these areas of your life.

How Positive Thinking Helps Your Relationships

Do you find yourself picking arguments over small issues? Do you have difficulty taking responsibility for your role in interactions? Do you tend to think the people around you can't grow and change? Do you isolate to avoid intimacy? These are just a few examples of how a negative mindset can infiltrate our relationships and set them on a destructive path.

You are more likely to attract significant others who have mindsets similar to yours. The more you can foster a positive mindset, the more you will attract others who do the same while also modeling this healthier path for your loved ones. Remember that it is not selfish to focus on your own mindset; it is actually a gift to others as well.

WHAT IS YOUR RELATIONSHIP TO POSITIVE THINKING RIGHT NOW?

Use this self-assessment to evaluate your present mindset. For each prompt, circle the response that you engage in more frequently. The column with the most circled responses will provide insight into your present relationship with positive thinking.

	NEGATIVE MINDSET	POSITIVE MINDSET
WHEN ONE THING GOES WRONG IN MY LIFE . . .	I tend to let it snowball into feeling like everything is going wrong.	I embrace it as a challenge to overcome and grow through.
WHEN I THINK ABOUT THE FUTURE . . .	I tend to think it looks bleak.	I tend to think it looks promising.
WHEN IT COMES TO TIME . . .	I always fixate on the past and/or future.	I give myself space to be in the present moment.
WHEN THINKING OF OTHERS . . .	I am more likely to criticize them.	I am more likely to compliment them.
WHEN MY PLANS BECOME INTERRUPTED OR SHIFTED . . .	I tend to get frustrated.	I tend to be easygoing.

The Benefits of Positive Thinking

Let's shift gears and discuss all that you have to look forward to: the numerous, life-changing benefits of positive thinking! To understand these benefits, it's important to know that your mental and physical health are interconnected. Therefore, your mindset and ability to stay positive play a huge role in both your mental and physical well-being.

Numerous Health Benefits

When it comes to physical health, research has found that positive thinking decreases cortisol, the stress hormone in the brain that leads to health issues. Levels of cortisol impact immune system function and heart health. Positive thinking can help strengthen your immune system and heart function, while decreasing your vulnerability to illness, including the common cold. Furthermore, positive thinking can alleviate, or even stop, psychosomatic symptoms, which are physical pains like stomachaches, muscle pain, or heart palpitations that arise from distressing feelings. To top it all off, positive thinking can even increase your life span.

Yup, you read that right: Positive thinking helps you live longer. Your mind and body are intimately connected—one could even say they are the same thing—and when you train your mind to be more positive, your body will be healthier.

Stress Management

The tools for positive thinking presented in this workbook will allow you to cope more efficiently during distressing times and decrease your overall stress.

As we discussed, the hormone cortisol activates feelings of stress in your mind and body. High levels of stress can impact your sleep, motivation, sex drive, emotional regulation, and much more. Shifting one's mindset from negative to positive decreases cortisol levels, alleviating the negative side effects of stress. It's a true mental game changer.

Better Relationships

Another incredible benefit of positive thinking is that you can improve your relationships with yourself and others. With positive thinking, you'll embrace more empathy and compassion, which leads to feeding your own emotional needs and cultivating healthy communication with others. This leads to a decrease in impulsive, harmful behaviors and an increase in more balanced, healthy behaviors, which will help you foster and maintain healthier, more aligned relationships.

Live a Happier, More Fulfilling Life

Research indicates that shifting to a positive mindset leads to higher feelings of life satisfaction, feelings of happiness, hopefulness, resiliency, and self-esteem. Furthermore, positivity mobilizes you to achieve your goals in a kinder, more impactful way. When we push ourselves using criticism and rigidity, we're much less likely to have confidence and are prone to closing our minds to more flexible, creative ways of thinking. A positive mindset allows us to feel more capable, fulfilled, and open.

These are only some of the many benefits that positive thinking has to offer. You will find your own benefits as you shift your mindset and behaviors. These benefits are limitless, and they can transfer into every single aspect of your life. All it takes is you making a commitment to yourself to practice, to be compassionate to yourself, and to be patient. You can do this.

Challenges You May Face Along the Way

It's always good to consider what challenges could be ahead when starting any new venture. So here you'll learn about some of the challenges you may face when embarking on the positive mindset journey.

Meta-Judgment

Struggling with a negative mindset means that you're prone to self-criticism and self-judgment. Something that I found from my experiences and those of my clients is that, once you begin to actively recognize and name your self-judgment, you will then begin to judge your own judgment. I like to call this "meta-judgment." Meta-judgment keeps us caught in the cycle of negativity. But don't you worry! You'll learn more about how to manage meta-judgment later in this workbook.

Backdraft

Have you ever started self-work only to find that you end up even more critical of yourself? This is backdraft showing up. The term "backdraft" was coined by a leading researcher of self-compassion, Dr. Kristin Neff, and is defined as a release of pain that comes when you start to show yourself kindness, understanding, and authenticity. Shifting your mindset involves facing pain that you likely haven't made space to fully feel. It can be a bit unnerving. Just remember that this is a normal part of the process and will become easier with time and practice.

Grief

Another common challenge my clients face when they begin the positive mindset journey is grief. I'm not talking about grief in the traditional sense of loss or death, but rather the mourning that shows up when you realize how negativity has immensely impacted your life in heartbreaking ways. It hurts to realize how much a negative mindset has held you back. The good news is that you are showing up for yourself now and shifting your mindset for the better. It's never too late.

Pushback from Others

Yet another challenge you may face is pushback from significant others in your life. Sometimes family members, romantic partners, friends, or coworkers may become jealous of the positive changes they begin to see you go through. Sometimes they may be scared of losing the idea of who they thought you were. They could be afraid they'll lose the comfort of what your relationship brings them when you are in a more negative mindset. This may not be intentionally malicious (in fact, I'd say in most cases it isn't), but it still can be tempting for us to return to our more negative ways of thinking when loved ones are pressuring us to do so. Remember that, in healing yourself, you are ultimately helping them, too.

You Won't Become an Optimist Overnight

I truly wish there was some magical overnight cure to help you shift your mindset. But the truth is, that doesn't exist. As mentioned earlier in this chapter, it takes time and patience to rewire your brain. It takes time to decondition the negative messages that you have internalized. Just know that the more you think and behave in ways that foster compassion and positivity, the more your brain will rewire to a more positive mindset. Every victory counts, no matter how small. Know that this practice is so worth the benefits and that you are very much worthy of this journey.

Positive Thinking Can Change Your Life If You Let It

What's the key to all of this? You. This doesn't mean you have to be alone on the journey. But it does mean that you are the only one who can shift your mindset. No one can force you to change. You are in control of your mind's destiny. You must commit to your healing if you want to see positive change. All you have to do is take a chance on yourself—a beautiful, life-changing chance.

Conclusion

I am proud of you for picking up this book and beginning your commitment to positive thinking! You've already learned the foundations. Take a moment of appreciation for simply showing up for yourself. That's no small feat. In chapter 2, we'll dive even further into this empowering journey. You'll begin to learn some manageable, tangible strategies for how to shift toward a positive mindset in your day-to-day life.

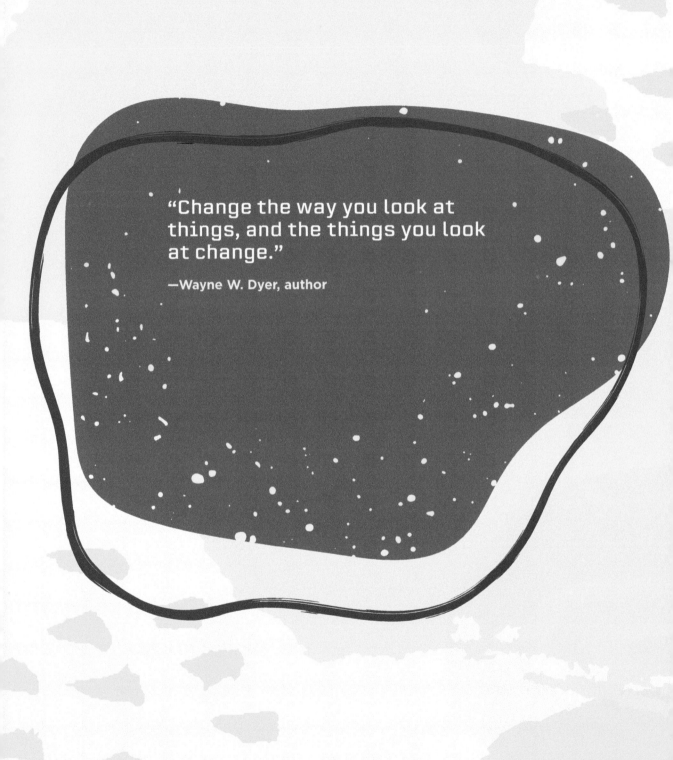

"Change the way you look at things, and the things you look at change."

—Wayne W. Dyer, author

CHAPTER TWO

PREPARE TO SHIFT YOUR MINDSET

Woohoo! You made it to chapter 2! Take a moment to check in with yourself. What thoughts are showing up for you? What emotions are you experiencing? What's happening in your body? Honor whatever shows up for you. There are no right or wrong answers to these questions. Also, surprise! You just practiced a positive mindset tool. Positive mindset tools can be as simple and accessible as a quick check-in.

There may be a few things that surprise you on this journey. In this chapter, you'll learn what to expect and how to put into practice what you learn. By the end of this chapter, you should feel ready to jump into the process.

Lean In to Positive Thinking

As you learned in chapter 1, research shows that there are many life-changing benefits to positive thinking. The more you can lean in to positive thinking, the more you will benefit from it. Your thoughts, emotions, and behaviors are all intimately connected and influence one another. The more you dive into positive thinking, the more you will experience pleasurable emotions and engage in healthy behaviors, then those emotions and behaviors will help further boost your positive mindset. It is a virtuous cycle. But what will this actually look like in practice?

It Won't Mean You Are Always Happy and Upbeat

When shifting your mindset, it's important to allow yourself the space to feel *all* of your emotions, including the distressing ones. Why? Because in order for your emotions to not fester and compound inside of you, you need to feel them rather than repress them. This may not be the answer you want to read. Of course, it would be lovely to remove any and all distressing emotions and only feel the pleasurable ones. Unfortunately, it's simply impossible to do so.

In fact, when you push away your distressing emotions and do not provide yourself the space to feel them, you are actually hurting yourself. You bottle them up inside of you. The more you do that, the more damage you do to your inner and external worlds. These trapped emotions begin to show up as psychosomatic symptoms, relational issues, harmful behaviors, and explosive reactions. Imagine a soda can. What happens when it's shaken before it's opened? The pressure builds inside. As it continues to be shaken without being opened, the pressure begins to exceed the space it's given. Eventually, it explodes. The same goes for our emotions.

But you also don't want to overindulge your distressing emotions. Doing that can lead to overidentifying with your emotions, which feeds them. Overindulgence can look like self-talk that encourages your emotions to become even stronger. An example of this would be telling yourself "I am a total failure" when you're feeling incompetent. In contrast, a healthy balance looks like a space between suppression and overindulgence that allows you to feel what's happening in your body and mind before letting the emotion pass. You'll learn some tools for emotional balance later on in this workbook.

What this means is that you won't always feel your 100-percent best. There are days that will feel crappy. Let yourself feel it. This doesn't mean you're failing at positive thinking. It actually means you're embracing it with kindness, understanding, and the right coping strategies.

It Won't Mean You Never Have Sad, Hard, or Difficult Thoughts

Just as you can't permanently get rid of distressing emotions, you won't be able to completely rid yourself of negative thoughts. Remember how I told you about the biological, evolutionary purpose of negativity in our brains? Yup, it's in our nature. But that's not to say you can't reduce these challenging thoughts or begin to overcome them with more ease. You totally can, and this book will help you. The tools we'll cover will teach you to start noticing these thoughts as brain output instead of truth. Remember, you shouldn't believe everything you think. You will also be able to move forward from these thoughts with more efficacy, rather than getting stuck in them. And the more you practice, the easier it gets.

It Will Mean You Become More Attuned to Your Thinking

Here's a nugget of wisdom to remember: Awareness of your thoughts is the first step toward shifting your mindset. During this process, you're going to get really close and intimate with your thinking patterns. You're going to develop insight into how your thoughts show up and why they show up in the ways that they do. This attunement is going to allow you to make significant changes in your mindset. It's a gift to be able to attune to your thoughts. However, awareness alone won't shift your mindset. It will take thoughtful and compassionate action in conjunction with attunement to make these shifts.

It Will Mean You Develop Productive, Positive Strategies for Handling Life

Shifting to positive thinking will help set you up for success. You will establish tools to add to your resilience toolbox that you can pull from any time life gets challenging. You will have different types of tools to manage different scenarios. With practice, you'll find that your ability to manage difficult, stressful situations will increase profoundly. You'll have direction when things get tough; annoyances will slip off you more easily; your productivity will increase; you'll maintain happier, healthier relationships; and your goals will be realized, one by one.

Make Time to Sit with Your Thoughts

When guiding my clients on the positive thinking journey, I have found that they show a lot of resistance to taking time for themselves. It's understandable. I have struggled with this, too. We all lead super busy lives. We want to be there for our families, careers, friendships, creative ventures, and more. Our capitalistic society has conditioned us to prioritize our external world over our internal world, and it's normalized to be on the go at all times. In fact, it may even feel uncomfortable for you to begin allowing yourself to focus on your own thoughts. Resistance will likely show up. Your ego may tell you that it's selfish to focus on yourself. Remember that you are worthy of this time. Remember that the time you feed yourself will feed others.

A Few Minutes Is Better Than Nothing

I do want to acknowledge that it is a privilege to be able to take time out of your day to focus on yourself. I practiced therapy with low-income, underprivileged populations for a number of years. There are people out there who can barely take time in their day for themselves because they have to work multiple jobs, go to school, and take care of their family. They have to lead that nonstop life to simply survive in this world. If you have the privilege of being able to take some time for yourself, please embrace it. It is a gift.

If you are someone who is struggling to make ends meet, remember that a few minutes a day is better than nothing at all, even if that means simply taking some deep breaths on your work break or checking in with your five senses before you fall asleep. Even the smallest moments make a difference.

THREE POSITIVE-THINKING HACKS

1. **View positive thinking as an experiment.** Be curious. Don't get caught up in trying to be perfect at having a positive mindset. Instead, try to think of positive thinking as an experiment. This will help you maintain more curiosity, flexibility, and motivation.

2. **Prioritize the areas of your life that you want to focus on.** You may feel overwhelmed when beginning this journey. I recommend making a list of areas you want to focus on (e.g., body image, career, relationship) and then prioritizing one or two areas to start.

3. **Take small steps.** Don't try to take on too much at once. Start small. You're more likely to continue this journey if you're successful at small steps.

Simple Ways to Practice Positive Thinking Every Day (Beyond This Book)

In the rest of this workbook, you'll learn specific tools that will help you develop positive thinking. However, below are some more general ways that you can develop a positive mindset in your day-to-day life.

Mindfulness

Mindfulness is one of the most helpful tools to foster a positive mindset. Mindfulness is the practice of being in the present moment without judgment. If you've attempted this skill before, you have likely found that it's easier said than done. However, when you bring gentle awareness to your experiences without judgment, you are cultivating valuable insight while allowing your brain the space to process your experiences. This means noticing your internal experiences of thoughts, emotions, and bodily sensations, while also noticing your external experiences of what's happening in your immediate environment.

Often, our minds are consumed with the future or the past. It can be rare to find ourselves living in the present moment. Perhaps you ruminate on things that have already happened, or perhaps you get caught up in what the future holds. Perhaps you struggle with both. Just know that the more awareness you can bring to the present experience without judgment, the more you are able to foster a positive mindset.

Meditation

Meditation, a formal practice of mindfulness, is the practice of training your attention through active awareness and focus on stimuli (e.g., your breath, your third eye, your body, or mantras). There is a huge misconception about meditation that you may hold. Most people think that in order to meditate, they are not allowed to think or feel. This is simply not true. Meditation is about noticing the thoughts and feelings that arise and then bringing your attention to whatever the meditation has you focusing on. It's completely normal to experience thoughts when meditating; even the most experienced meditators can't completely block out their thoughts.

My clients often share that they become frustrated with thoughts during meditations, because they thought the goal was to not think. However, when they learned that the practice was about awareness and attention rather than not thinking, their whole experience shifted. I encourage you to try it out. Meditation is a brain muscle that needs to be exercised. It will get easier with practice, and the mental benefits are huge!

There are many different types of meditations out there: guided, unguided, mindfulness-based, spiritually based, and more. Go on the internet and explore your options to find what works best for you.

Visualization and Guided Imagery

Visualization and guided imagery are powerful tools for enhancing a positive mindset. Visualization involves using your mind's eye to literally visualize whatever you are imagining. Guided imagery involves using your mind's eye to immerse all five of your senses (sight, sound, smell, taste, and touch) into whatever you are imagining.

Visualization and guided imagery can help you in a multitude of ways. They can be used to help you relax, process different scenarios, and manifest your goals. For example, in a time of stress, you may immerse yourself in imagery of a beautiful forest to help you find serenity. Or, if you were trying to decide between two different job offers, you might try visualizing two different futures for yourself. My suggestion is to get creative with it. Let it be fun!

Breathing and Breathwork

Breathing is something we don't usually notice. You may even take your breathing for granted. How often do you check in with your breath? Breathing is a source of power. It is your life force. It anchors you to the present moment. Furthermore, it gives you insight into what you may be feeling in that moment.

Start by simply noticing your breath. Attune yourself to how you experience your breath in your body. Notice its pace and depth and see where you can feel it the most in your body. When you feel stressed, your breath is likely shallow, fast-paced, and situated in your chest. When you feel calm, your breath is likely deep, slow-paced, and reaching your belly. The act of noticing can help us regulate our brains toward more positivity.

Additionally, you can consciously control your breathing to facilitate a positive mindset. This is known as breathwork. There are different types of breathwork that you can practice. I encourage you to research different types of breathing techniques and see what works best for you. One of my favorites is placing one hand on your belly and breathing into it, commonly known as diaphragmatic breathing or "belly breathing."

Breathing techniques help you regulate your autonomic nervous system. Therefore, these techniques help regulate other physiological functions, including your heart rate and blood pressure, and they can decrease distressing emotions and defuse the fight-or-flight response. Who knew that something so simple could be so profound?

Body Awareness and Body Scan

Just as connecting to your breath can significantly impact your mindset, so can connecting to your body. Take a moment to consider how often you are attuned to your body. If you're like the majority of people, you probably don't check in with your body very frequently. As you become aware of your body's experiences, you'll connect to your inner experience and make room for whatever is showing up for you.

A body scan is an incredible tool that can allow you to check in and align with your body. It's a practice in which you bring gentle awareness to each part of your body. It can be helpful to close your eyes and start at one end of your body, either the top of your head or the bottom of your feet. Bring a soft awareness to this area, noticing how this part of your body feels, and then slowly begin scanning either up or down your body to bring awareness to other areas. Notice any judgments that arise. Simply take note of them and bring your attention back to the body scan. The goal is to tune in to all areas of your body.

You can choose to notice what you feel in your body without trying to change it, or you can attempt to change that experience. You might relax distressed areas of your body by breathing into them, or you might squeeze tense muscles and then release them to allow them to relax. Both practices are extremely helpful for fostering awareness, acceptance, and peace of mind.

Gentle Movement (Yoga, Stretching, Walking, and More)

We all know that working out is good for our health. But did you know that you don't always need fast-paced, heart-pumping activities to support your vitality? In fact, slower, more gentle practices are just as important to our well-being. Gentle movement impacts both your physical and mental resilience. There are many ways you can practice gentle movement. Some examples include yoga, stretching, walking, tai chi, free-form dancing, and chair exercises. Again, find what works best for you!

Physical activity is often viewed as a chore. Societal norms internalize this idea that physical activity means that you must go to the gym for 45 minutes, four times a week, every week. I just want you to know that *all* forms of physical activity and *any* duration of time spent being active are valid. Please find what physical activity brings you joy. Don't settle for anything less.

Journaling

Journaling is a great way to process your feelings and shift your mindset. There is no right or wrong way to journal. To be honest, I am not a natural journaler. But when I do journal, I realize that it is incredibly powerful. I notice an immediate shift in my mood. My clients report this experience as well. You can write down a few words or a whole book. It doesn't matter. Just see what shows up for you. Writing helps you externalize the negative thoughts and/or distressing emotions, fosters insight, and improves your ability to process them. Try it out and see if it helps!

HOW DOES POSITIVE THINKING SHOW UP IN YOUR LIFE?

Use the self-assessment below to determine which areas of your life you tend to think about with more positivity and which areas of your life you struggle to think about with positivity. Then, identify three areas of your life in which you would like to increase your positive thinking.

Using the scale below, rate the frequency of positive thinking for these different areas of your life:

1 = Never • **2** = Rarely • **3** = Sometimes • **4** = Occasionally • **5** = Frequently

_____ I feel good about my family dynamics.
_____ My romantic life is fulfilling or will be one day.
_____ I am happy in my present friendships.
_____ I am satisfied in my career or feel like I am on the right path.
_____ I do not have much stress around my finances but still pay attention to them.
_____ I make time and space for creative outlets/hobbies.
_____ I feel I am generally smart/competent.
_____ My health isn't a huge concern, but I am still mindful of it.
_____ I feel good about the amount of physical exercise that I engage in.
_____ I rarely have negative thoughts about my body image.
_____ My spiritual/religious life is fulfilling.

Lower scores indicate that you engage in less positive thinking in that specific area of your life, whereas higher scores indicate that you engage in more positive thinking in that specific area of your life. Ideally, to have a well-rounded positive mindset, your scores would fall in the range of 3 to 5.

Three areas in which I can foster more positive thinking:

1. _____

2. _____

3. _____

Please know that the purpose of this assessment isn't to induce shame. Be honest with where you are at while knowing that it's okay to struggle in these areas. Remember, your brain has been wired to be negative, both biologically and environmentally. Show yourself grace. You are already taking profound steps toward a more positive mindset!

You Will Learn to Have a New Outlook on Yourself and the World around You

This journey may be a challenge, but it is profound. With practice, you'll start to notice harmful thoughts and habits drift away. You'll also begin noticing a significant shift in your worldview. You'll see your inner strength and resilience grow. You'll feel empowered. You'll experience more moments of joy. You'll live more authentically. You won't rely as much on others' opinions and the conditioned social responses that were ingrained in you. This is very powerful healing and self-work. You are nourishing your outlook and doing this, in turn, nourishes your whole self. Don't take this lightly. Know that even the smallest shifts in your outlook will make significant ripples in your life.

Remember to Take It Day by Day

Similar to the process of addiction recovery, it is very helpful to take this journey one day at a time. Looking too far in the future or having expectations that are too high will likely lead to feelings of disappointment, and disappointment is one of the biggest demotivators. In fact, small steps rather than big leaps are more likely to lead to long-term success. Start small and stay in the present. You will face setbacks and you will have times where it feels impossible. You may feel like giving up, but don't. Know that your well-being depends on it and that you are beyond worthy of all the benefits that positive thinking has to offer.

Let's Get Started

Get excited! In the second part of this book, you'll be able to apply all this life-changing knowledge and put it into tangible action. There are over 130 tools and practices for you to work with. Take your time. See what works best for you. Grasp onto the pieces that resonate with you. This is an exciting journey!

Conclusion

Perhaps you're feeling really excited for this journey, or perhaps you're feeling overwhelmed. Maybe you're feeling both! Show yourself some love for jumping in. Do a little dance. Release. Now, let's begin practicing some positivity.

By meeting myself where I am at, I am setting myself up for success.

2

A ROAD MAP FOR POSITIVE THINKING

We're going to take all the life-changing information you just learned and put it into practice! In part 2, each chapter will present you with a variety of prompts, exercises, practices, and affirmations to help you fully embrace positive thinking in your day-to-day life. You will dramatically increase your self-awareness, use tools to soothe your inner critic, shift your mindset, learn to embrace gratitude, and foster resilience via social support and daily practice.

Remember that these tools require consistency to be effective. Try to be patient with yourself. Take your time. You don't have to do this overnight. In fact, you can't do this overnight. But I promise you there is some significant positive change that comes with this commitment to your wellness.

"The seed of suffering in you may be strong, but don't wait until you have no more suffering before allowing yourself to be happy."

—Thich Nhat Hanh,

The Heart of the Buddha's Teaching

CHAPTER THREE

CHECK IN WITH YOURSELF

I'm so proud of you for making it here! This chapter is going to help you garner a sense of where you're currently at in your mindset. You'll be checking in with different areas of your mind, body, and soul through writing prompts, exercises, affirmations, and practices. By the end of this chapter, you will have a solid understanding of how much you currently embrace positive thinking. The goal is to foster acceptance of where you are and let go of any judgments you may be holding on to. Know that you are on this healing journey for a reason and that it doesn't matter where you started—it just matters that you started.

Positive Mindset Assessment

Let's start with a positive mindset assessment to identify your starting point. Circle the response that best represents your relationship to the statements provided.

1. **During my day, I take time to be mindful (present in the moment without judgment).**

    1. Never
    2. Rarely *(circled)*
    3. Sometimes
    4. Usually
    5. Almost Always

2. **I engage in positive self-talk when I need encouragement.**

    1. Never
    2. Rarely *(circled)*
    3. Sometimes
    4. Usually
    5. Almost Always

3. **I show myself self-compassion (understanding and kindness) when I don't meet expectations set by myself or others.**

    1. Never *(circled)*
    2. Rarely
    3. Sometimes
    4. Usually
    5. Almost Always

4. **I recognize my thoughts aren't necessarily fact, and I don't believe everything I think.**

    1. Never
    2. Rarely *(circled)*
    3. Sometimes
    4. Usually
    5. Almost Always

5. **I forgive myself when I make mistakes.**

    1. Never
    2. Rarely *(circled)*
    3. Sometimes
    4. Usually
    5. Almost Always

6. **I communicate my needs to others in healthy ways.**

    1. Never
    2. Rarely
    3. Sometimes *(circled)*
    4. Usually
    5. Almost Always

7. **I try to maintain flexibility in my life, as I understand that life isn't linear.**

   1. Never
   2. Rarely *(circled)*
   3. Sometimes
   4. Usually
   5. Almost Always

8. **I let myself feel my emotions without suppressing or overindulging them.**

   1. Never
   2. Rarely
   3. Sometimes
   4. Usually *(circled)*
   5. Almost Always

9. **I take time to ask myself where my negative thoughts come from.**

   1. Never
   2. Rarely *(circled)*
   3. Sometimes
   4. Usually
   5. Almost Always

10. **I acknowledge and nurture my mind-body-soul connection.**

    1. Never
    2. Rarely *(circled)*
    3. Sometimes
    4. Usually
    5. Almost Always

11. **When looking back at the past, I recall and acknowledge the positive moments I have experienced.**

    1. Never *(circled)*
    2. Rarely
    3. Sometimes
    4. Usually
    5. Almost Always

12. **I have optimism about and hope for the future.**

    1. Never
    2. Rarely *(circled)*
    3. Sometimes
    4. Usually
    5. Almost Always

13. **I believe that people (including me) can change.**

    1. Never
    2. Rarely
    3. Sometimes
    4. Usually *(circled)*
    5. Almost Always

Add up the scores from each of your answers using the scale below:

Never = 0 point

Rarely = 1 points

Sometimes = 2 points

Usually = 3 points

Almost Always = 4 points

Q1 _2_ + Q2 _2_ + Q3 _1_ + Q4 _2_ + Q5 _2_ + Q6 _3_ + Q7 _2_ + Q8 _4_ + Q9 _2_ + Q10 _2_ + Q11 _1_ + Q12 _2_ + Q13 _4_ = Total ___

0 to 25 = Positive Mindset Novice

If you scored in this range, you're likely struggling with prominent negative thinking. Don't let this get you down! By actively using the tools presented in this workbook, you'll be set up to rewire your brain to embrace positivity!

26 to 36 = Positive Mindset Apprentice

If you scored in this range, you already have some positive mindset tools under your belt. Awesome! You are going to keep building on these skills and, with practice, will quickly become a pro.

37 to 52 = Positive Mindset Pro

If you scored in this range, you already engage in some radical positive thinking. Congrats! You're set up to apply these skills in all areas of your life via this workbook!

Now that you've been presented with all the knowledge from the previous two chapters and have evaluated your current positive mindset, what thoughts do you have about starting this journey? What is your current motivation level, on a scale of 0 to 10? What are the reasons you feel this way? Assessing yourself at each stage of this journey is a mindfulness practice in itself and will help nurture positivity!

_____

_____

_____

_____

_____

Let's check in with your mind and body. Notice how you are feeling. What emotions are you experiencing? What sensations do you feel in your body? Try not to judge your experience, but if judgment does show up, that's totally okay and normal. Write down whatever shows up. Quick check-ins like these help foster mindfulness and positivity.

_____

_____

_____

_____

_____

My Current Self-Care Assessment

This assessment helps you gauge your current relationship with a range of self-care activities. After completing the assessment, you'll identify three areas you'd like to improve.

Using the scale below, rate the frequency of the following self-care:

1 = Never
2 = Rarely
3 = Sometimes
4 = Occasionally
5 = Frequently

_____ Favorite hobbies
_____ At least seven hours of sleep each night
_____ Joyful physical activity/exercise
_____ Rest and breaks
_____ Preventive care and other medical care as needed
_____ Nourishing eating
_____ Healthy coping skills for stress
_____ Healthy boundaries with others
_____ Socializing with friends
_____ Spending time in nature
_____ Cleaning my environment
_____ Vacationing/taking time off
_____ Wellness rituals (showers, massages, skin care, etc.)
_____ Healthy media consumption

Three areas to begin improving:

1. _____

2. _____

3. _____

How will embracing positive thinking personally change your life? What are some of the benefits that you hope to see? You can always come back to this response to motivate you throughout this work.

_____

_____

_____

_____

_____

What are your expectations for yourself on this journey? Remember, setbacks are to be expected. How can you maintain a realistic outlook and address any perfectionism that arises?

_____

_____

_____

_____

_____

THE FIVE A'S OF MINDFULNESS

The Five A's of Mindfulness is a powerful tool to guide you in gentle awareness and self-compassion in your day-to-day life. The goal is to use this five-step tool when distressing thoughts come to mind. It will help you move away from emotional reactivity, cultivate mental clarity, and engage in kind action. Simply follow the steps below and be sure to softly notice any judgment that arises.

1. **Awareness:** When a distressing thought, situation, or emotion arises, notice and become aware of what is showing up for you. This can include noticing what is happening physically in your body, noticing emotional reactivity, and noticing what is happening in your immediate environment.

2. **Acknowledgment:** Name or label whatever is showing up for you. This can include labeling your emotion(s), labeling your thought(s), labeling what you are feeling in your body, and naming the present situation (sad feelings, tense muscles, self-critical thoughts, judgment, etc.).

3. **Acceptance:** Meet yourself where you are. Offer yourself the understanding that whatever is showing up for you is okay and will pass. This can include allowing yourself to feel, trying not to judge what is showing up for you, not pushing past the emotion/thought/situation, and acknowledging why you may be feeling distress.

4. **Appreciation:** Find it within to offer yourself appreciation. Appreciate the fact that your body and mind are trying to help you by signaling distress. This is an opportunity that is allowing you to heal and grow. This can include acknowledging that this is an opportunity to learn more about yourself, understanding that difficult emotions ultimately serve a kind purpose, and bringing awareness to the fact that you are attempting to heal in this moment. (This is for sure the most difficult step. Try to be patient with yourself. This takes practice!)

5. **Action:** Ask yourself, "How can I take care of myself in this moment?" and develop a compassionate action plan. This can include asking yourself what would be helpful in the situation, seeking support, engaging other helpful coping skills, self-care, and more.

Remember, this will take time to master. You are rewiring your brain, and it takes consistent practice to do so. This way of thinking will get easier the more you engage with it. Believe in yourself. Know that it's so worth the challenge.

THE PARADOX OF RADICAL ACCEPTANCE

In his book *On Becoming a Person: A Therapist's View of Psychotherapy*, Carl Rogers philosophized, "The curious paradox is that when I accept myself just as I am, then I can change." For most of us, it feels unnatural to accept ourselves fully at this moment in time. We are taught that acceptance will lead to stagnation, hold us back from success, and demotivate us from achieving our goals. In reality, radically accepting all parts of ourselves is necessary for positive change in all these areas. It leads us to believe more in our ability, encourage ourselves, and take confident risks. When you catch yourself saying that you can't accept yourself, remind yourself of this paradox.

Having support from others is integral to fostering and maintaining a positive mindset. Identify one or two people who can help support you on this journey. This can be a trusted friend, a dependable family member, or a wellness professional like a therapist, coach, or counselor.

_____

_____

_____

_____

_____

Mindful Breath

In this short exercise, you will connect with your breath. The purpose of this activity is not to change your breath but to notice what it feels like in this moment. Your responses can provide insight into how you may be feeling, as your breath is connected to your nervous system, which regulates the physiology of your emotions.

Circle the response that corresponds to your present breathing:

My breath feels . . . SHALLOW or NORMAL or DEEP

The pace of my breath is . . . FAST or NORMAL or SLOW

I most significantly feel my breath in my . . . CHEST or NOSE or STOMACH

If your responses were shallow, fast, and/or chest breathing, this may indicate that you are experiencing higher levels of stress and anxiety. In this case, check in with your emotions and ask how you can take care of yourself in this moment. If your responses were deep, slow, and/or stomach breathing, this may indicate that you are experiencing lower levels of stress and more feelings of calm. Wonderful! Ask yourself what you have been doing prior to this exercise that increased these feelings for you.

What did you learn about emotions when you were growing up? Who or what overtly or covertly taught you these messages (family, media, religion, societal norms)? Has your view of emotions changed over time? If yes, how have these messages changed? Why did they change? Insight into your emotional history will allow you to understand your emotional patterns and empower you to unlearn unhealthy messages.

_____

_____

_____

_____

_____

_____

_____

_____

_____

_____

_____

_____

Sitting with Thoughts and Feelings

In this True/False exercise, you'll examine whether you tend to suppress, overindulge, or balance different types of thoughts and feelings. Circle True or False for each statement.

Suppression of thoughts and feelings:

True/False I push away and minimize any <u>happy thoughts</u> that arise.

True/False I push away and minimize any <u>stressful thoughts</u> that arise.

True/False I dismiss and ignore <u>uncomfortable feelings</u> like anxiety and depression.

True/False I dismiss and ignore <u>positive feelings</u> like moments of joy and pleasure.

True/False In general, it is more comfortable for me to <u>distract myself from thoughts</u>.

True/False In general, it is more comfortable for me to <u>hide and bottle up my emotions</u>.

Analyze your results. If you found that you answered True to most of these questions, you tend to engage in suppression of thoughts and emotions. With this knowledge, begin to attempt to honor and sit with your feelings by feeling where they are in your body or by journaling about them.

Overindulgence of thoughts and feelings:

True/False I tend to overindulge my <u>negative thoughts</u> and catastrophize situations.

True/False I tend to overindulge my <u>positive thoughts</u> and engage in toxic positivity.

True/False I tend to <u>fake positive emotions</u> or make things seem positive even when they aren't.

True/False I tend to <u>work myself up and exaggerate uncomfortable emotions</u>.

True/False In general, it is more comfortable for me to <u>overthink and believe all of my thoughts</u>.

True/False In general, it is more comfortable for me to <u>latch on to my emotions for long periods of time</u>.

Analyze your results. If you found that you answered True to most of these questions, you tend to engage in overindulgence of thoughts and emotions. With this knowledge, begin to examine what thoughts and behaviors you engage in that overindulge your emotions. Consider creating a list to foster further awareness.

Balance of neither suppressing nor overindulging thoughts and feelings:

True/False I sit with <u>positive thoughts</u> that arise without dismissing them or engaging in toxic positivity.

True/False I sit with and breathe through <u>negative thoughts</u> that arise and let them pass naturally.

True/False I sit with <u>positive emotions</u> that arise without suppressing them or engaging in toxic positivity.

True/False I sit with <u>distressing emotions</u> by letting myself feel them, breathing through them, and letting them pass naturally.

Analyze your results. If you found that you answered True to most of these questions, you overall tend to engage in a healthy balance of feeling your thoughts and emotions! Bravo! With this knowledge, consider how you can continue to practice emotional balance in your life.

In what areas of your life do you already engage in positive thinking? Why is it easier to maintain more positivity in these areas? In what areas of your life do you struggle to maintain a positive mindset? Why is it more difficult to maintain positivity in these areas? Looking at the areas of your life where positive thinking is easy can help you identify ways to embrace positive thinking in more difficult areas of your life.

_____

_____

_____

_____

_____

_____

_____

_____

_____

_____

_____

_____

BODY SCAN

The practice of a body scan is a great way to check in with your bodily sensations and aid in awareness. You can practice a body scan anywhere and at any time. However, if you're at home, I recommend setting up an inviting environment for you to practice in. This can mean lighting a candle, playing relaxing music, or turning the lights low—do whatever makes you feel in tune with yourself. During the practice, your attention may shift away as distracting thoughts arise. Simply notice the thoughts and gently return to the body scan practice.

To practice, follow the steps below:

1. Sit with your feet on the ground or lie down in a comfortable position in which you can maintain stillness as much as is physically possible for you.

2. Gently close your eyes or bring your gaze softly downward.

3. Take three deep breaths into your belly.

4. Turn your attention to the very top of your head. What does it feel like? What sensations arise?

5. Slowly begin scanning downward. Scan all parts of your face (forehead, eyebrows, eyes, cheeks, and nose) one at a time. Notice any areas of tension or any areas of relaxation.

6. You may notice internal and external sensations. Whatever shows up for you is completely valid.

7. Continue scanning downward, bringing your gentle awareness into your neck and then your shoulders. Your sensations may change as you bring awareness to them; however, try not to intentionally change anything about your experience. Simply try to notice it.

8. Next, begin scanning down your arms into your hands and then into your fingers.

9. Notice any judgments about your experiences that may arise as you are scanning. Acknowledge these judgments and allow them to pass.

10. Softly shift your awareness around to the top of your back and begin scanning downward. Again, notice any sensations without intentionally trying to change anything.

11. Then wrap your attention around to the top of your chest. Begin scanning downward into your sternum, upper abdomen, belly, and pelvic region. You may observe the sensations of your breath in these areas.

12. Begin scanning down your thighs and into your knees, calves, and ankles.

13. Bring your awareness into your feet and toes.

14. Finish off by becoming aware of your entire body as a whole, simply noticing and sitting with whatever shows up for you.

15. Take three deep breaths into your belly.

16. Wiggle your fingers and toes and softly open your eyes when you are ready.

When finished, take a moment to acknowledge how the body scan experience was for you. Whatever showed up for you is completely normal and valid. With practice, focusing your attention will become easier.

Self-Acceptance of Parts of Self

In this exercise, you'll explore three parts of yourself that you dislike or view as weaknesses and three parts of yourself that you like or view as strengths. It's important to begin accepting all parts of yourself as you shift to positive thinking. These reflection questions will help you move toward a more accepting approach to yourself.

List three parts of yourself that you like or view as a strength:

1. _____

2. _____

3. _____

How did you learn these were likable or strong?

_____

How does it feel for you to acknowledge these likeable and/or strong areas/identities?

_____

List three parts of yourself that you dislike or view as a weakness:

1. _____

2. _____

3. _____

Where did you learn that these were unlikeable or weak?

_____

How have these areas actually served to help or protect you in life?

_____

Acknowledging how these areas have been instrumental in protecting you will help foster self-compassion. Perhaps they have been overindulged or harmful, but there has been a purpose behind them. Acknowledging this and offering these parts of yourself kindness will aid in self-acceptance. Remember, self-acceptance doesn't mean you can't change!

What does your self-talk sound like? Do you tend to encourage yourself and speak to yourself kindly? Do you tend to engage in self-critical or even hostile thoughts? Self-talk is critical to your positive mindset journey. Getting a baseline will help you determine how to move forward.

_____

_____

_____

_____

_____

_____

_____

_____

_____

_____

_____

_____

12 WAYS TO INSTANTLY GROUND YOURSELF

When awareness arises, anxiety and self-judgment may arise as well. Grounding techniques are helpful tools you can use to bring yourself back to earth in these moments. Here are 12 grounding techniques to rapidly decrease stress and shift your mindset in these moments:

1. Place an aromatherapy oil under your nose.

2. Lie down on the floor and immerse yourself in the pull of gravity.

3. Describe an object in your space in full detail. (You can do this in your mind or in writing.)

4. Take a cold shower.

5. Listen to your favorite song.

6. Go for a walk in nature.

7. Feel the sensations in the bottoms of your feet.

8. Make and drink a cup of tea.

9. Pet an animal.

10. Write down your thoughts.

11. Clench and release your fists.

12. Read words backward, letter by letter.

Identifying Common Setbacks

Below is a list of common setbacks that you may face when trying to embrace positive thinking in your life. Use the blank lines to list the areas of your life these setbacks tend to show up in. Having this knowledge fosters awareness and increases your likelihood of recognizing and addressing these setbacks as they arise on your positive mindset journey.

Procrastination
Area(s) of your life this shows up in: _____

Shying away from risk
Area(s) of your life this shows up in: _____

Negative self-talk
Area(s) of your life this shows up in: _____

Lack of consistency
Area(s) of your life this shows up in: _____

Toxic positivity
Area(s) of your life this shows up in: _____

Isolation
Area(s) of your life this shows up in: _____

Perfectionist standards
Area(s) of your life this shows up in: _____

Caring too much about others' opinions
Area(s) of your life this shows up in: _____

Distractions
Area(s) of your life this shows up in: _____

Lack of balance
Area(s) of your life this shows up in: _____

What negative self-perceptions and self-narratives do you hold? Where did you learn these perceptions and narratives? Remember, you are not born with these narratives. They have been learned. By identifying your self-perceptions and self-narratives, you can begin to embrace the ones that are helpful and shift the ones that are harmful.

_____

_____

_____

_____

_____

_____

_____

_____

_____

_____

The Mindful Five Senses Checklist

One of the best ways to check in with yourself is to mindfully connect with your five senses. Use the checklist below to practice and reflect on your experience. It's okay if you can't taste or smell anything at the moment. Simply note whatever experience shows up for you. This will help you shift your mindset when you're feeling in need of a mental break.

☐ **Vision.** Check in with what you see around you.

Colors I see include: _____

Objects I see include: _____

☐ **Hearing.** Check in with what you hear around you.

Sounds from far away I can hear: _____

Sounds from within the room I can hear: _____

Sounds from within my body I can hear: _____

☐ **Taste.** Check in with what you can taste.

Tastes I can sense: _____

☐ **Smell.** Check in with what you can smell.

Smells that I can sense: _____

☐ **Touch.** Check in with what you can feel around you.

Different textures I can feel: _____

Your relationships are impacted by your mindset. What do your current relationships look like? Do you tend to isolate yourself or over-enmesh with others? Are you able to set healthy boundaries? Awareness of your boundaries helps you gain insight into how your present mindset is impacting your relational dynamics. This may provide you with even further motivation to heal and grow!

_____

_____

_____

_____

_____

_____

_____

_____

_____

_____

Affirmations for Motivation

As you start to dive deeper into these practices, it will be helpful for you to engage in motivational self-talk on the journey. Here you will think of some areas where you may need some encouragement to stay motivated. Then you will identify positive affirmations to use both preventively (before things get tough) and when the struggle shows up.

One area you may struggle in (example: body image):

_____

An affirmation you can use (example: My body is worthy of respect.):

_____

One area you may struggle in (example: career):

_____

An affirmation you can use (example: I will overcome any obstacles that show up.):

_____

One area you may struggle in (example: anxious thoughts):

_____

An affirmation you can use (example: I do not have to believe my anxious thoughts.):

_____

Creative Visualization

Visualize yourself at the completion of this workbook. What does your life look like? What behaviors are you engaged in? In what ways has your life changed? How have your relationships shifted? What does your environment look like? This will allow you to foster motivation for continuing your positive mindset journey.

Use the space below to draw a picture that represents your visualization.

Conclusion

What new areas of awareness have you opened up in your mind, body, and soul? Know that no matter where you are, you are exactly where you need to be. You are not behind. You are not failing. You are not a lost cause. You are learning. You are growing. You are healing. Next, you are going to learn how to use all this awareness and healing energy to befriend your inner critic.

"We already have everything
we need. There is no need
for self-improvement . . .
all the time our warmth
and brilliance are right
here. This is who we really
are. We are one blink of
an eye away from being
fully awake."

—Pema Chödrön,
Start Where You Are: A Guide to Compassionate Living

CHAPTER FOUR

SOOTHE YOUR INNER CRITIC

Your inner critic can be a pain in the you-know-what. Am I right? What if I told you that befriending this foe was the only way to freedom? Don't run away. This isn't a trick! In this chapter, you'll learn strategies to garner insight into your inner critic and befriend it. From thoughtful prompts to cognitive tools to practices of radical acceptance, there is an array of tools you can use to embrace your inner critic. It may feel unnatural at first to offer your inner critic kindness, but over time you will start to see how this kindness soothes and heals your inner critic. And just as a reminder, you can't completely get rid of your inner critic or your negative thoughts, but you certainly can reduce those negative thoughts with these tools.

Befriending your inner critic can be a challenging task. When you think of doing so, what shows up for you? Do you notice any resistance to this idea? If so, what is behind this resistance? Awareness of your present resistance can help you notice and manage future resistance.

_____

_____

_____

_____

_____

Typically, the inner critic comes out when you make a mistake or don't live up to an expectation. What does your inner critic say to you in these moments? Do you call yourself names? How can you start to bring in more self-compassion in these moments?

_____

_____

_____

_____

_____

5-4-3-2-1 Grounding

Sometimes your inner critic can become so overwhelming that it feels impossible to soothe. Fortunately, this easy mindfulness tool can help you in these moments. It can help regulate your brain to move it away from distressing thoughts and into logical thinking. Let's practice right now!

Below, you'll write down each step. However, in your daily life, you can do this practice mentally, making it available anytime and anywhere.

5: Identify five things that you can see.

1. _____
2. _____
3. _____
4. _____
5. _____

4: Identify four things that you can touch.

1. _____
2. _____
3. _____
4. _____

3: Identify three things that you can hear.

1. _____
2. _____
3. _____

2: Identify two things you can smell.

1. _____
2. _____

1: Identify one thing you can taste.

1. _____

You can repeat this exercise as needed until the stressful thoughts pass.

As a child, what did you learn about worthiness? What did you learn about shame? How do you connect this to your present feelings of worthiness and shame? Identify where you learned these different values from. Should these perceptions be harmful or unhelpful, this awareness will allow you to begin separating yourself from them.

_____

_____

_____

_____

_____

_____

_____

WHAT IS TRAUMA?

You've likely heard the term "trauma," but what is its true definition? Trauma is an emotional response that occurs after a highly distressing event. This can be an event that you directly experienced, an event you witnessed, or an event that you heard about (also known as "vicarious trauma"). Trauma can be acute (short-term), chronic (long-term), or complex (multiple compounded traumas). Trauma impacts one's mind and body. Symptoms of trauma can include panic, intrusive memories, sleep disturbances, dissociation, intense distress, impaired memory, hypervigilance, difficulty concentrating, and irritability. Trauma is individualized, meaning not everyone may experience trauma from the same events. Trauma can amplify your inner critic and impact your relationship with yourself. If you believe you are suffering from debilitating trauma symptoms, please reach out for professional support. There is no shame in doing this. It is an act of self-compassion. (You'll find suggestions in the resources section at the end of the workbook.)

Reconstructing Shameful Trauma Narratives

Trauma can play a huge role in how you view yourself. Do you find that you blame yourself for trauma(s) you've experienced? Did you feel guilt or shame after your experience? This is a very common response after trauma. I've worked with many survivors of sexual assault, intimate partner violence, and traumatic loss. Most, if not all, of my clients have experienced these emotions, which then led to a need for control and perfectionism. Below, you will identify a trauma that has impacted your life and reconstruct your role in the situation. This will allow you to separate yourself from the narrative and give you space to foster a new, healthier one.

Identify a trauma you've experienced:

_____

_____

Describe any feelings of guilt, blame, or shame stemming from this experience:

_____

_____

Identify any overt or covert messages you received from others that made you feel at fault for this trauma:

_____

_____

Identify any resulting perfectionistic/controlling behaviors and rigid thought patterns you've adopted since:

_____

_____

Reconstruct this narrative by identifying why you were not at fault for this trauma:

_____

_____

THE RAIN TECHNIQUE

Originally developed by Buddhist teacher Michele McDonald and then adapted by author and psychologist Dr. Tara Brach, the RAIN technique will help you nourish more positivity in your mindset when your inner critic shows up or when you experience distressing emotions. This is accomplished through mind-body awareness. Follow these steps to practice this self-compassionate tool in your daily life:

R: Recognize What Is Happening

The first step is to recognize your thoughts and emotions. What sensations are present in your body? What belief is showing up for you?

A: Allow Life to Be Just as It Is

Allow yourself to sit with whatever is showing up for you. Do not try to change your experience. You can use an affirming statement here if it helps. For example, you can say, "I let this moment be."

I: Investigate with a Gentle, Curious Attention

Using a soft curiosity, begin to investigate your experience of what is coming up for you. This can include: What is the most difficult part of this emotion/belief/thought? Have you experienced this emotion/belief/thought before? What do you need in this moment?

N: Nurture with Loving Presence

Identify what compassionate action you can take to nurture yourself. Befriend your experience. Offer it kindness. Take thoughtful action, whether it be internal or external.

In what ways do you hold yourself to different standards than those you apply to others? Are the standards you set for yourself realistic? Often, we're unaware of how high our self-standards are until we compare them to the standards we hold for others. You may consider shifting your self-standards to look more like the ones you hold for others.

_____

_____

_____

_____

_____

Primary vs. Secondary Emotions Quiz

Primary emotions are the initial emotions you experience after a thought or situation. Secondary emotions are the resulting emotions that you feel as a response to the primary ones. These two categories of emotions can be exemplified by reactions to a surprise party: The primary emotion would be feeling surprised and letting out a loud squeak. The secondary emotion would be feeling embarrassed about your squeak.

It's helpful to be able to differentiate between primary and secondary emotions. Why? Although you cannot stop yourself from feeling your emotions, you can shift the secondary emotional response via self-care or mindfulness practices when you are aware of it. Doing this ultimately fosters positivity. Take the quiz below to see if you can differentiate between primary and secondary emotions. An answer key follows.

1. Feeling startled after witnessing a car accident. PRIMARY or SECONDARY

2. Feeling sad about the lack of deep relational connections in my life after a boring conversation. PRIMARY or SECONDARY

3. Feeling angry after a boss shamed you in front of coworkers. PRIMARY or SECONDARY

4. Feeling joy when listening to your favorite song. PRIMARY or SECONDARY

5. Feeling fear that you will be punished after yelling at someone. PRIMARY or SECONDARY

6. Feeling disgusted after watching someone dehumanize a loved one. PRIMARY or SECONDARY

Answer key: 1 = primary, 2 = secondary, 3 = secondary, 4 = primary, 5 = secondary, 6 = primary

Think of a recent challenging situation. How did you approach this situation? In what ways could you have approached this situation with more compassion and positivity? As you analyze past challenges, you can help better prepare yourself for future ones.

_____

_____

_____

_____

_____

_____

_____

_____

Self-compassionate reframing is when we take a self-critical thought and shift our perspective and/or narrative to one of kindness and understanding. This allows us to heal and motivates us to move forward with thoughtful, compassionate action.

Below you will find a "thought log" in which you will identify a self-critical thought, note where that message originally came from (the external source), explore the function of that thought (what it is actually doing for you), and come up with a self-compassionate reframe. This is a skill that takes practice. You can use the examples below as a guide. Remember to be gentle with yourself on this journey.

Self-Compassionate Reframing: Thought Log

Self-Critical Thought	External Source	Function of the Thought	Self-Compassionate Reframe
"I really suck at life. I eat crappy food, I don't work out nearly enough, and I look gross."	Family told me I was never an acceptable size. Media representation made me feel my body wasn't desirable. Friends always talked about never working out enough.	Keeps me from taking risks, as it keeps me comfortable in my current patterns. Also, keeps me caught up in consumer culture.	"It has been hard for me to take care of myself because I was taught to view it as a chore instead of self-care."
"I am not worthy of self-compassion. I need to be hard on myself if I want to change and be successful."	Individualistic society that emphasizes criticism as a form of motivation. Modeled by my parents.	Protects me from external judgment. I'm trying to preempt what I perceive others think about me.	"I am worthy of the same compassion I show to others. Self-compassion will not impede me and will actually motivate me toward change and achieving my goals."

Self-Critical Thought	External Source	Function of the Thought	Self-Compassionate Reframe

How does your inner critic hold you back? How does it impact your motivation and/or success? Getting to know your inner critic will help you change your relationship to it.

_____

_____

_____

_____

_____

Creative Externalization of Your Inner Critic

Close your eyes and imagine that your inner critic popped out of your body. What does your externalized inner critic look like? Perhaps it looks like an intimidating monster, a super villain, or some abstract entity. Picture your inner critic in full detail. How big is it? What color is it? What textures does it have? Where does it impact your body?

Draw an image of your externalized inner critic below:

Next, close your eyes and imagine yourself befriending this externalized inner critic. In what ways would you attempt to befriend it? As it begins to respond to your kindness, how would its appearance change? Picture this shift in appearance in great detail.

Now, draw an image of your befriended inner critic below:

What does this practice teach you about befriending your inner critic?

_____

_____

Our negativity toward ourselves consequently impacts others around us. In what ways
does your inner critic negatively impact others in your life, such as family, friends,
coworkers, or strangers? With this insight, you may find more motivation to shift your
relationship with negativity.

_____

_____

_____

_____

_____

Breathing Through Distress

This tool aids in emotional balance when distressing thoughts or emotions present themselves. It allows your brain to process the emotion and allows you to not suppress it or overindulge it. Just like all mindset-shifting activities, this tool takes practice. This exercise will give you the opportunity to practice and to reflect on this technique.

To begin, think of a situation that brings you mild to moderate irritation. Don't choose anything too infuriating or traumatic, as it's best to start small. With practice, you can use this technique with more intense situations and feelings.

Situation: _____

Next, identify where in your body you're feeling this emotion.

_____

Continue to sit with this emotion and place your hand on your belly. Begin breathing deeply into your belly (rather than your chest) until the emotion naturally passes.

What was your experience of this technique?

_____

_____

_____

_____

In what ways do you treat yourself differently from those whom you love? Think of a recent shortcoming you perceived in yourself and identify how you talked to yourself about this situation. Then identify what you would have said to a loved one in the same situation. Doing this will help you discover kinder words to use in your self-talk.

_____

_____

_____

Inner Critic Symptom Checklist

Below you'll find a list of symptoms you may experience when your inner critic is present. These symptoms can vary from person to person. Identifying your individual symptoms will help you become more mindful when your inner critic is present and embrace more compassionate self-talk. Check off the ones that specifically show up for you:

Physiological:

☐ Muscle tension

☐ Heart racing

☐ Heart palpitations

☐ Crying

☐ Fatigue

☐ Sweating

☐ Upset stomach

☐ Restlessness

☐ Shortness of breath

☐ Light-headedness

Psychological:

☐ Rigid thinking

☐ All-or-nothing thinking

☐ Anger/irritability

☐ Depression

☐ Anxiety

☐ Panic

☐ Fixating on the future

☐ Ruminating on the past

☐ Difficulty sleeping

☐ Difficulty concentrating

☐ Mind racing

☐ Indecisiveness

Behavioral:

☐ Impulsive behaviors

☐ Obsessive behaviors

☐ Lashing out at loved ones

☐ Yelling

☐ Cursing

☐ Hitting/punching things

☐ Binge eating

☐ Isolation

☐ Procrastination

☐ Avoidance

☐ Hypervigilance

As you learned earlier in this workbook, your inner critic can take the form of backdraft, or the negative thinking that can arise as you begin embracing a more positive mindset. Has backdraft shown up for you thus far? If so, what has that looked like and how have you managed it?

_____

_____

_____

_____

_____

_____

_____

_____

_____

_____

_____

Deconstructing Sources of Self-Perceptions

Across our lives, we internalize overt and covert messages that we receive from external sources, such as our family and the media. In this exercise, you'll identify different messages you received about your different identities and passions across your life. You'll also consider where these messages came from. Then you'll summarize how these messages impacted your self-perceptions. Externalizing these messages and acknowledging that you were not born with these messages will help you begin to decondition any messages of shame that you received.

For example, at the intersection of gender and family, someone may say, "My family taught me that being a womxn meant that I couldn't be loud." Likewise, at the intersection of race and media, an example would be writing, "Lack of POC representation taught me that my skin color wasn't desirable." In the table below, write in the messages that you've learned about your different social identities from various sources.

Consequential internalized messages:

→ What I learned about my gender from external sources was . . .

_____

_____

_____

→ What I learned about my race from external sources was . . .

_____

_____

_____

→ What I learned about my sexual orientation and romantic relationships from external sources was . . .

_____

_____

_____

→ What I learned about my body image and ability from external sources was . . .

_____

_____

_____

→ What I learned about my life path/career from external sources was . . .

_____

_____

_____

→ What I learned about my hobbies, interests, and passions from external sources was . . .

_____

_____

_____

Just because you're moving toward more self-kindness doesn't mean that you can't still be honest and acknowledge your mistakes. How can you be honest with yourself without being self-critical? What can you tell yourself so that you can let go of judgment?

_____

_____

_____

_____

_____

	Gender	Race	Sexual Orientation and Romantic Relationships	Body Image and Ability
Family				
Friends				
Media				
Religion/ Spirituality				
Cultural Background				
Other Social Norms				

SES (Socioeconomic Status)	Life Path/Career	Hobbies, Interests, and Passions

Write a Letter to Your Inner Child

Your inner child holds the unconscious childlike responses that have developed due to past experiences of unmet needs and childlike awe. This part of yourself can be playful, innocent, sensitive, fearful, and resentful. It's most helpful to think of your inner child by simply imagining yourself as a child. This part of you, just like a child, needs kindness, nurturing, and compassion. Use this space to write a letter to your inner child. (If you have access to a childhood picture of yourself, look at it before you write your letter.) Showing your inner child kindness and compassion will allow you to decrease negativity and increase positive thinking.

_____

_____

_____

_____

_____

_____

_____

_____

_____

_____

_____

_____

_____

_____

_____

_____

_____

_____

WERE YOU PARENTIFIED AS A CHILD?

From my experience with friends, families, and clients, I have found that a significant number of us were "parentified" as children. What does this mean? It means that we engaged in a role reversal in which, as children, we had to take on a role of parental responsibility toward ourselves, our family members, or even our own parents. We took care of others (emotionally, physically, or psychologically) when we needed to be taken care of. This often means that our own parts of self that needed vital nourishing were left unnurtured, which, unfortunately, likely led to perfectionistic tendencies and unhealthy boundaries. Take a moment to reflect on whether this was your experience. By taking care of your inner child now, you can help reverse these negative impacts of parentification.

OBSERVING YOUR THOUGHTS: AN IMAGERY MEDITATION

The meditation below is a creative tool for you to practice witnessing your thoughts and letting them go. In this meditation, you will use imagery to help you imagine thoughts passing with ease. This practice will help strengthen positive mindset pathways in your brain. You may practice this meditation sitting or lying down.

1. To begin, gently close your eyes.

2. Take three deep breaths in and out.

3. Shift your attention to the center of your head.

4. Begin to imagine you are in nature, sitting against a tree along a creek. What type of tree is it? What does this tree look like? How big is it?

5. Imagine hearing the wind rustle the leaves of the tree. Notice the temperature in this environment. Take note of what else is around you in this space.

6. If you haven't already imagined it, what does this creek in front of you look like? What sounds does it make? How fast is it moving?

7. Simply be aware of this creek. Gently focus your attention on it.

8. Now, as thoughts begin to arise, notice them passing by on this creek, coming into view as they show up and gently drifting out of view as they pass down the creek. Perhaps they float by on tiny boats or logs. You can imagine this part however you like.

9. Continue to engage in this practice for as long as you like.

10. When you are ready, let go of this image and return to your breath.

11. Take three deep breaths in and out.

12. Wiggle your fingers and your toes to come back into your body, and when you are ready, gently open your eyes.

After completing this practice, acknowledge to yourself if it was easy or challenging for you to let go of your thoughts on this creek. Whatever showed up for you is completely valid. Honor your experience and know that, with rehearsal, this practice becomes easier.

I am worthy of the self-work it takes to befriend my inner critic and cultivate joy.

Conclusion

Now that you have insight into your inner critic and have begun using tools to soothe it, have you noticed your self-compassion increase at all? Or perhaps the opposite is occurring and backdraft is showing up for you. Either way, you should be really proud of yourself for making it through these exercises and practices. I am certainly proud of you. You're absorbing a lot of information, and you're embracing significant transformative shifts! Fortunately, there is plenty more to share as we dive deeper into shifting your mindset in the next chapter.

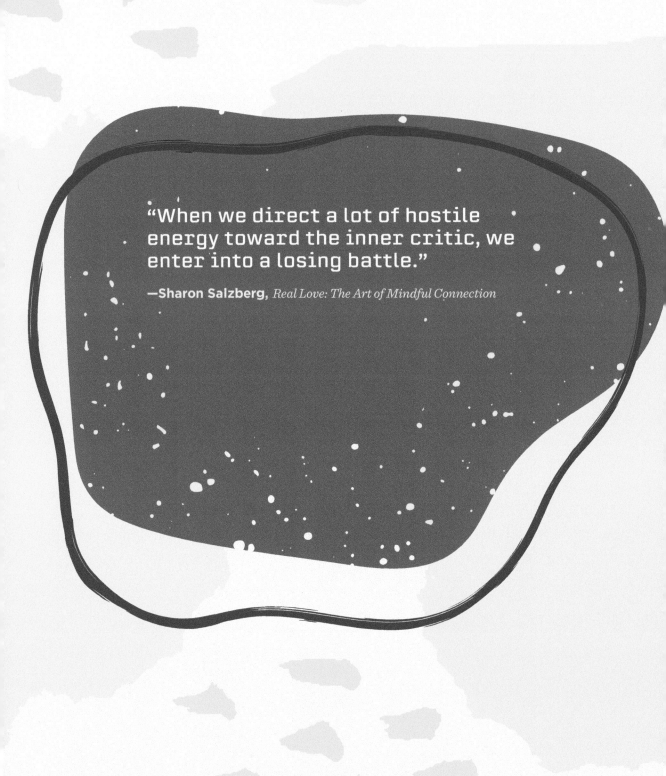

"When we direct a lot of hostile energy toward the inner critic, we enter into a losing battle."

—**Sharon Salzberg,** *Real Love: The Art of Mindful Connection*

CHAPTER FIVE

SHIFT YOUR MINDSET

Shifting your mindset isn't a linear process. Likely there will be ups and downs along this journey. However, the more you dive into these practices and engage with these tools, the more you will see the incredible benefits of positive thinking. Remember, self-compassion is truly vital on this journey.

As you're working through this section, be aware of any self-criticism that arises. If you start judging your responses, remember that no one is perfect and that we all have failed, made mistakes, and struggled in life. Offer yourself some understanding and kindness. You have been so resilient across your life. This section will help you foster this astounding resilience in healthier and more empowering ways.

Flexibility Assessment

Flexibility and adaptivity are key to shifting your mindset. How flexible are you in your day-to-day life? How well are you able to adapt and change? Here you will assess your ability to foster flexibility in your life. Your results will provide insight into your thought patterns and highlight potential areas for improvement.

1. **When I need to unexpectedly adjust my plans, I tend to feel exasperated.**

   1. Never
   2. Rarely
   3. Sometimes
   4. Usually
   5. Almost Always

2. **I like being unconventional in my approaches to life.**

   1. Never
   2. Rarely
   3. Sometimes
   4. Usually
   5. Almost Always

3. **I tend not to take risks or try new things unless forced.**

   1. Never
   2. Rarely
   3. Sometimes
   4. Usually
   5. Almost Always

4. **I've been told that I'm amenable and easygoing.**

   1. Never
   2. Rarely
   3. Sometimes
   4. Usually
   5. Almost Always

5. **When someone cancels on me at the last minute, I feel very frustrated.**

   1. Never
   2. Rarely
   3. Sometimes
   4. Usually
   5. Almost Always

6. **I find it exciting to try new things, even when I'm unsure of the outcome.**

   1. Never
   2. Rarely
   3. Sometimes
   4. Usually
   5. Almost Always

7. **I like to maintain a strict routine, and I become flustered when it's interrupted.**

   1. Never
   2. Rarely
   3. Sometimes
   4. Usually
   5. Almost Always

8. **Surprises tend to make me feel happy and excited.**

    1. Never
    2. Rarely
    3. Sometimes
    4. Usually
    5. Almost Always

9. **I've been told that I'm set in my ways.**

    1. Never
    2. Rarely
    3. Sometimes
    4. Usually
    5. Almost Always

10. **I am able to change my views and opinions when presented with new information.**

    1. Never
    2. Rarely
    3. Sometimes
    4. Usually
    5. Almost Always

11. **Once I'm set on something, it's hard to change my mind.**

    1. Never
    2. Rarely
    3. Sometimes
    4. Usually
    5. Almost Always

12. **When confronted with a challenge, I think of multiple creative ways to overcome it.**

    1. Never
    2. Rarely
    3. Sometimes
    4. Usually
    5. Almost Always

Use the scale below to add up the scores for questions 1, 3, 5, 7, 9, and 11:

Never = 0 point

Rarely = 1 points

Sometimes = 2 points

Usually = 3 points

Almost Always = 4 points

Q1___ + Q3___ + Q5___ + Q7___ + Q9___ + Q11___ = Total₁ ___

Use the scale below to add up the scores for questions 2, 4, 6, 8, 10, and 12:

Never = 4 point

Rarely = 3 points

Sometimes = 2 points

Usually = 1 points

Almost Always = 0 points

$$Q2\_\_\_ + Q4\_\_\_ + Q6\_\_\_ + Q8\_\_\_ + Q10\_\_\_ + Q12\_\_\_ = Total_2\_\_\_$$

Now sum up these scores:

$$Total_1\_\_\_ + Total_2\_\_\_ = Final\ Score\_\_\_$$

Interpreting your score:

0 to 12 = Flexible and Adaptable

If you scored in this range, you likely display flexibility and adaptability with ease in your life. Kudos! This is no easy feat. Consider how you can continue to display this level of flexibility moving forward in your positive mindset journey.

13 to 35 = On the Way to Flexibility

If you scored in this range, you may have some flexibility tools under your belt but haven't fully embraced them yet. Perhaps you are flexible in some areas and rigid in others. That's okay. You're on the right track!

36 to 48 = Stuck in Rigidity

If you scored in this range, you likely struggle with the practices of flexibility and adaptability. There is no need to have hard feelings about scoring in this range. Rigidity is a form of protection. Please honor where you are at while also challenging yourself to embrace more flexibility moving forward.

When unexpected challenges arise, do you find it easy or hard to adapt? Give at least three reasons for your answer. By clarifying your responses to challenges, you'll be better set up to respond in healthier ways.

_____

_____

_____

_____

_____

_____

_____

_____

_____

_____

_____

Remaining Present

As you've learned, practicing cognitive awareness of your experience is critical to shifting your mindset. Take a minute to close your eyes and tune in to your mind and body to simply notice your experience right now. Then note what shows up for you below.

Areas of tension in your body: _____

Areas of relaxation in your body: _____

Areas of pain in your body: _____

Areas of neutrality in your body: _____

Current emotionality: _____

Current motivation level: _____

Current mental activity: _____

Are you judging any of your present experience? YES or NO

Now offer yourself a statement of kindness for whatever is showing up for you: _____

Typically, how do you manage your own failures and shortcomings? What thoughts and behaviors show up for you in these situations? By recognizing your thoughts and behaviors, you'll increase awareness and be able to respond in more thoughtful ways.

_____

_____

_____

_____

_____

What are some areas in which you hold a rigid mindset? Why is it understandable that you've held these rigid cognitions? What are some ways you can foster more flexibility?

_____

_____

_____

_____

_____

_____

_____

_____

_____

_____

Language Matters

As you've learned, the way you talk to yourself plays a huge role in your mindset. Actively noticing critical wording will allow you to begin shifting to kinder approaches. Below are some areas of language to begin shifting and reflections to help you begin practicing.

Should/Shouldn't: Telling yourself you "should" or "shouldn't" be doing something often comes from a place of judgment.

Is this a type of self-talk you tend to engage in? **YES or NO**

What is an example of how this self-talk shows up for you?

_____

What's a kinder way to approach self-talk in these areas?

_____

Always/Never: Saying "I always" or "I never" is another form of self-talk that can be limiting and rigid.

Is this a type of self-talk you tend to engage in? **YES or NO**

What is an example of how this self-talk shows up for you?

_____

What's a kinder way to approach self-talk in these areas?

_____

Label-First vs. Person-First Language: It can be helpful to shift the way you address yourself when discussing your identities and labels. For example, if you say you are an "anxious person," you're placing the label first. If you say you are a "person who experiences anxiety," you're placing your person first. Why does this matter? Label-first language tends to place your whole identity on one part of yourself and can compound the meaning that part of you holds in your life. Person-first language helps you acknowledge that you are a multifaceted person who has many identities and parts that make up your whole self.

Do you tend to engage in label-first language? **YES or NO**

Identify one label-first phrase you have held about yourself:

_____

Shift this phrase to person-first language:

_____

Dehumanizing Language: Dehumanizing language is any cruel, harsh, or mean words or phrases you use to describe yourself or talk to yourself. This can include curse words.

Is this a type of self-talk you tend to engage in? **YES or NO**

What is an example of how this self-talk shows up for you?

_____

What's a kinder way to approach self-talk in these areas?

_____

MINDFUL LANGUAGE: YES AND NO

How many times do you say "yes" to taking small risks? How many times do you say "no" when others ask you for help? Are you keeping yourself in a box and/or straining yourself by saying "yes" or "no" too frequently? Becoming aware of the patterns and reasons behind your "yes" and "no" responses is important to facilitating a more positive mindset. With this insight, you can challenge yourself to change your answer, should you find that you're limiting yourself or burning out due to your response patterns. Try saying "yes" to beneficial risks and help from others if this is something you normally avoid. Try saying "no" to unhealthy interactions and overextending yourself. Be mindful in your approach to set yourself up for success.

MINDFUL MOVEMENT

Mindful movement is an active way to embrace mindfulness in your day-to-day life. You do not have to be still and seated to practice mindfulness and meditation. In fact, using mindful movement will increase your ability to shift your mindset when you're on the go and don't have time to sit down. All you have to do is tune in to your five senses (sight, smell, sound, taste, and touch) during these activities.

Below are some mindful movement practices for you to try out:

→ **Walking meditation:** Take a walk and become fully immersed in the environment around you. Notice the different colors you see. Feel the air on your skin. Listen to the birds chirping. Allow yourself to be one with nature.

→ **Mindful chores:** Most of the time, our minds race as we are engaging in our everyday responsibilities, thinking of all that we need to do next. Instead, stay present with your senses when completing these tasks, including doing the laundry, showering, cleaning dishes, dusting, and brushing your teeth. Notice how this transforms your experience of the task itself.

→ **Dancing meditation:** Meditate on your body's experience of dancing. Notice how the movement makes the different areas of your body feel. Become aware of any emotional shifts that occur during your dance.

→ **Mindful cooking and eating:** Become immersed in the sights, sounds, and aromas when you're cooking. Then be fully present with each bite as you taste your creation and feel the textures in your mouth. Notice what it feels like to chew and swallow.

→ **Mindful exercise:** Allow yourself to be present when engaging in activities and exercise. Yoga is the prime example of how to stay mindful during exercise, as you are made to focus on your body. However, you can be mindful in any form of exercise, including more high-intensity activities.

→ **Mindful art hobbies:** Most of the time, when someone creates art or enjoys a hobby, they're already engaged in a mindful process. I suggest finding a creative outlet or hobby that calls to you. Notice if you're able to stay present with your choice.

→ **Mindful music:** Whether you perform or listen to music, you can find mindful moments through musical engagement. If you play an instrument, you can notice what it feels like to touch your instrument. If you sing, you can notice what it feels like to meditate on your own voice. If you only listen, you can notice the variety of notes that show up and be aware of any emotions that arise.

Know that you can engage in mindfulness during any part of your day no matter what you are doing. You can even have mindful conversations with others. All it takes is a little presence with your five senses. Enjoy this practice! It can be fun, calming, and joyful when you allow yourself to let go.

Challenging Rigidity

You can challenge your rigid or unchanging thoughts by fostering insight into the reason(s) why they may be present, as well as through perspective-taking. Below you'll identify a rigid thought you have about a situation in your life and a negative self-perception that you hold about yourself. You'll use the prompts to begin garnering understanding and shifting your mindset around these rigidities. Remember that it takes patience and practice using these tools to begin seeing long-term change.

Rigid Thought:

1. Identify a rigid thought you hold about a situation in your life.

_____

2. How does holding this rigid thought serve to protect you?

_____

3. How may someone else perceive this situation differently from you?

_____

4. Brainstorm alternative ways to view this situation and write them below.

_____

_____

_____

Negative Self-Perception:

1. Identify a negative self-perception you hold about yourself.

_____

2. Where did you learn this negative self-perception from?

_____

3. What would a trusted loved one say to you if they knew you held this perception?

_____

4. What evidence suggests that your negative self-perception is *not* true?

_____

_____

_____

Identify a time when you thought something was going to go badly but ended up being a positive experience. What can you take with you from this experience?

_____

_____

_____

_____

_____

_____

_____

Identify your enduring life narrative(s). These are fixed ideas that you've held about yourself across your life. They may be positive or negative narratives that you hold about yourself. By identifying your current narrative, you can begin to shift any parts of it that may be negatively impacting you.

_____

_____

_____

_____

_____

_____

_____

_____

_____

_____

_____

_____

Self-Care Ritual Development

Self-care routines can be integral to your motivation and energy levels. By ritualizing them (making them a part of your daily life), you'll set yourself up for positive mindset success. I challenge you to start small and be flexible! You won't be perfect at this. Think of it as an experiment and a learning process. Below you'll identify different types of self-care you can integrate into your daily ritual. Additionally, you'll identify helpful components to keep you accountable. Generally, these should be tasks you enjoy engaging in and that provide you with gentle nurturing.

Physical activities: (example: a 20-minute mindful walk)

_____

Soulful activities: (example: 10 minutes spent journaling)

_____

Relaxation activities: (example: 20 minutes spent reading)

_____

Nourishment activities: (example: an energizing snack)

_____

Grounding activities: (example: a 5-minute meditation)

_____

Cleaning activities: (example: putting away laundry)

_____

Energizing activities: (example: listening to your favorite song)

_____

Social media/news boundaries: (example: no news/social media before noon)

_____

When I can engage in my self-care ritual(s):

_____

Where I can engage in my self-care ritual(s):

_____

Who will be involved in my self-care ritual(s):

_____

How I can hold myself accountable:

_____

A kind statement that I can tell myself if I miss a self-care ritual:

_____

What are some current negative perceptions that you hold about yourself? How does holding these perceptions hold you back from living a more positive life? This insight will allow you to begin to let go of negative perceptions and embrace more positive ones.

_____

_____

_____

_____

_____

_____

Cognitive Distortions

Cognitive distortions are negative thinking patterns you engage in that warp reality. Below you will learn about five common distortions and identify examples of your distorted thoughts. This will allow you to recognize distortions as they arise in the future and embrace new perspectives.

1. **Polarized thinking:** This distortion, also known as black-and-white thinking and all-or-nothing thinking, is the tendency to view situations in a binary of either/or. For example, you may believe that you must be perfect at every task you engage in; otherwise, you are a total failure. This is a distortion, as there is actually a gray area or middle ground that is being left out.

   One polarized thought I engage in: _____

2. **Overgeneralization:** This distortion involves taking one situation and applying it to all situations. For example, you may receive a criticism about your body from a family member and then believe that *all* people must feel the same way about your body.

   One overgeneralized thought I engage in: _____

3. **Mind reading:** This distortion is present when you assume what other people are thinking about you and/or a situation. For example, you may think that your partner is angry at you without them ever sharing that they are upset with you.

   One mind reading thought I engage in: _____

4. **Emotional reasoning:** This distortion is when you believe that your feelings are facts. For example, you feel disappointed in yourself and therefore determine that you must not be worthy of love. However, in reality, you are always worthy of love. Remember, you don't have to believe everything you think.

   One emotional reasoning thought I engage in: _____

5. **Personalization:** This distortion involves making a situation about yourself, whether it is blaming yourself or taking something personally. For example, you may assume that someone canceled their plans with you because you must have done something to make them upset. However, perhaps, the person canceled the plans due to a family emergency.

   One personalization thought I engage in: _____

SCARCITY VS. ABUNDANCE MINDSET

Has capitalism got you feeling like there aren't enough resources to go around? Do you feel you are in constant competition with others? If so, you are likely suffering from a scarcity mindset. This mindset makes you feel like you do not have enough (e.g., money, resources, attention, love) and that there is not enough out there for everyone. If you struggle with this mindset, it can be helpful to begin fostering an abundance mindset. This is a positive thinking tool for recognizing that there are enough resources to go around and that you do not have to be in competition to get what you need. Obviously, oppressed people do not always have access to the same resources as privileged others, so please consider helping others via donations and political activism if you are able.

Humans are naturally very resilient. In what areas of your life are you resilient on a day-to-day basis? Recognizing your everyday resiliencies shifts your mind into a more positive place!

_____

_____

_____

_____

_____

Container Exercise

Container exercises are useful for maintaining mindfulness, as they help you shift away from past ruminations and future projections. They allow you to "put away" these ruminations and projections until you are ready to process them in a healthy way. For example, you may "put away" certain traumatic memories until you can process them with a specialized trauma therapist. Here you will practice a container exercise with a mildly troublesome situation. It's helpful to start with smaller disturbances and move to larger ones with practice.

1. Close your eyes and imagine a container in front of you. It is strong, secure, and able to carry anything concerning, painful, or disturbing. What does the outside of it look like? Be as detailed as possible: What is it made of? What textures and colors are present? How is it decorated?

   _____

   _____

   _____

2. How does it open and close? How does it lock?

   _____

3. Open the container. It is comfortable enough to hold all experiences you place inside. What does it look like on the inside?

   _____

   _____

4. Note any positive feelings that arise in knowing that you can hold any troublesome circumstances in this secure container.

   _____

5. Identify a positive word or phrase that represents your container. Use this phrase any time you want to access your container.

   _____

6. Now think of one mildly troublesome experience and imagine placing it inside of the container. When you are ready, close the container and lock it.

7. Let go of this imagery. Identify any feelings that arose after you put this experience into your container.

_____

_____

Use this container to put away disturbing experiences and access them when you're ready to process them. Know that this container will always be there to help you in times of need.

Have you had any negative self-talk or judgment show up as you've been completing this chapter? If so, what has that looked like? What did you do when it showed up?

_____

_____

_____

_____

_____

_____

Shifting to a Positive Life Narrative

Below you will begin writing a new, positive life narrative that comes from a place of insight, understanding, and kindness. Use the information you've gathered from previous exercises to help guide you. Write from a place of resilience and empowerment. Highlight your strengths and accomplishments. It can be helpful to imagine you are writing an empowering autobiography about your life. Where did you come from? What did you overcome? How did you use that in your future?

_____

_____

_____

_____

_____

_____

_____

_____

_____

_____

_____

_____

_____

_____

_____

_____

_____

_____

_____

_____

BELLY BREATHING

Belly breathing (also known as diaphragmatic breathing) is an amazing tool to help regulate your nervous system, which in turn will help you shift your mindset. Some of the benefits of belly breathing include decreasing stress, increasing alertness, and allowing your body to release toxins with more ease. It's very common for us to engage in chest breathing, in which our breath is short and moves mainly in our chest. In this practice, you'll learn how to deepen your breath by moving it into your belly and taking control of its pace.

1. Start by simply noticing your breath as it is right now.

2. Place your hand on your belly.

3. Begin to take a deep breath into your belly. Let the air expand deep into your belly so that your hand begins to move outward with your belly. Once your belly is filled with air, you may fill the rest of your chest cavity with air as well. The goal is to first feel movement in your belly and then let it fill your chest.

4. Hold this breath for 4 seconds.

5. Begin to exhale by first slowly moving the air out of your chest. Then slowly exhale the rest of the air from your belly. The goal in this step is to first feel movement in your chest and then end with it in your belly.

6. Once you have exhaled, wait 4 seconds before you take in another breath.

7. Then repeat steps 3 through 6 as many times as you'd like. It can be helpful to start small and then increase the number of times you engage in belly breathing once your body gets used to the practice.

Let's check in with your motivation. Why is shifting your mindset important to you? What are the benefits of doing so?

_____

_____

_____

_____

_____

_____

_____

Manifestation Drawing

In order to further shift your mindset, it can be helpful to put your intentions and goals out into the universe. Below you will practice a form of manifestation through drawing.

Take a moment to close your eyes and imagine you're in a space where you've achieved your goals and fostered a more positive mindset. Be realistic, aligned, and intentional in your vision. Notice all the details come to life. What does your life look like? What feelings arise? Now say to yourself, "What I put out into the world, I am more likely to receive." Then open your eyes and draw what you imagined in the area below:

You may like to keep this drawing in a place where it will inspire you in your day-to-day life!

Conclusion

You are becoming more positive with each chapter you complete. With the tools in this chapter, you've taken great strides toward shifting your mindset! You're gaining significant insight into your patterns and taking active steps to shift them. How does it feel to make these shifts? Likely, it's been a challenge. Perhaps you've started to see the benefits. Remember, the challenge is so worth it.

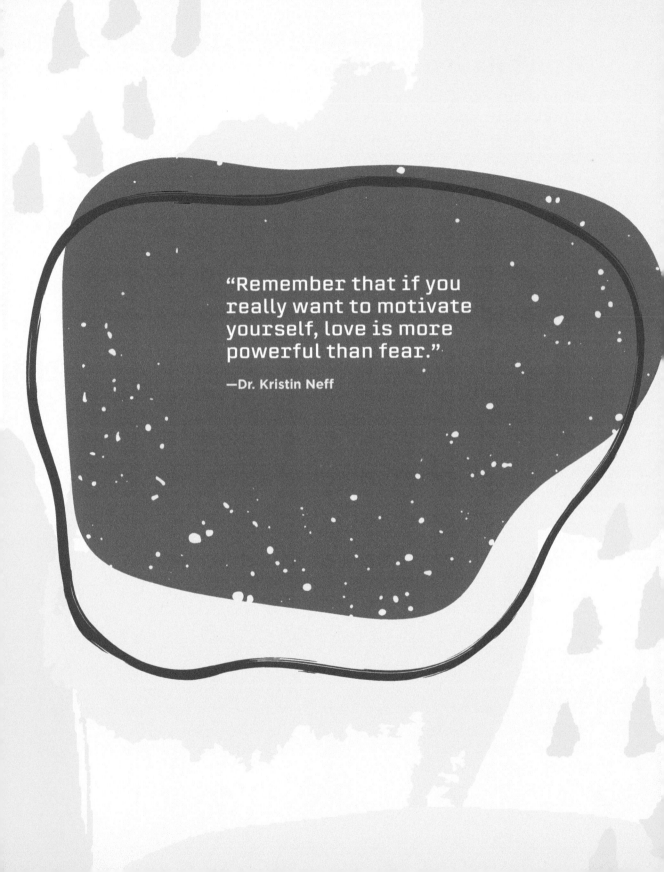

"Remember that if you really want to motivate yourself, love is more powerful than fear."

—Dr. Kristin Neff

CHAPTER SIX

EMBRACE GRATITUDE

How often do you experience and express gratitude in your life? You may be surprised to hear that gratitude is a practice. Most of us have to actively work at being grateful. Simply asking yourself to feel grateful isn't likely to do the trick. Just like any other positive thinking approach, gratitude requires rewiring of your brain with consistent practice. The tools in this chapter will help you cultivate a well-rounded practice of gratitude. Gratitude opens us up to positive thinking, aids our physical and mental well-being, increases happiness, and fosters healthier relationships. So, why not give it a try?

What shows up for you when you think about gratitude? Do you have resistance to accepting gratitude? How do you feel when others show you gratitude? How do you feel when offering yourself gratitude?

_____

_____

_____

_____

_____

_____

_____

_____

Gratitude Scale

Use the scale below to assess your current relationship with gratitude. Remember, gratitude isn't something we're naturally wired to feel, so you may not practice it very frequently. After you complete the scale, identify three areas in which you can foster more thanks. The more gratitude you can foster, the more joy you will find in your life!

Using the scale below, rate the frequency of the gratitude statements for you:

1 = Never
2 = Rarely
3 = Sometimes
4 = Occasionally
5 = Frequently

_____ I feel grateful every day.
_____ I have a lot to be thankful for.
_____ Overall, life has been worth living.
_____ I have a lot of people in my life I'm thankful for.
_____ I practice offering my body gratitude.
_____ I often feel thankful for the small things in life.
_____ I appreciate all of my emotions, even the distressing ones.
_____ I acknowledge the privileges in my life that others do not have.
_____ Whenever I am outside, I am in awe of nature's beauty.
_____ I am grateful for the hardships that have gotten me where I am today.
_____ I appreciate the good things that show up in my life.
_____ I can easily acknowledge my strengths.
_____ I acknowledge how resilient I've been over the course of my life.

For areas that you score in the 1 to 3 range, you may consider fostering more gratitude. Identifying these areas will help set you up for success.

Three areas in which I can foster more gratitude:

1. _____

2. _____

3. _____

In what ways do you express gratitude to your loved ones? Is this something you'd like to change? If so, how would you like to change it? How would it feel to turn this expression of gratitude inward?

Body Gratitude

One area that's easy to disregard is our own body. Most of us go about our day-to-day living without ever acknowledging our body's immense resilience and abilities. If you have undergone physical trauma or suffer from a disability, you've likely become more in tune with your body; however, you may or may not have been in the practice of expressing gratitude. It can be a challenge for some people—such as those who manage chronic pain or those who struggle with body image—to express gratitude to their bodies, but it's a practice that can truly cultivate inner peace. Use the image and prompts below to identify reasons you can be grateful for different areas of your body. Helpful hint: Think about the function of the body part and/or ways that it has overcome hardship in your life.

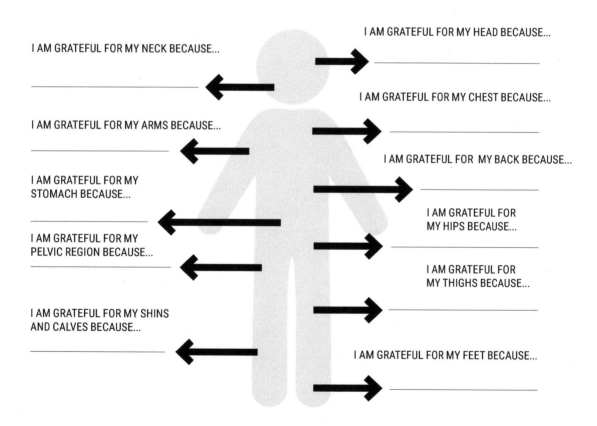

I AM GRATEFUL FOR MY HEAD BECAUSE...

I AM GRATEFUL FOR MY NECK BECAUSE...

I AM GRATEFUL FOR MY CHEST BECAUSE...

I AM GRATEFUL FOR MY ARMS BECAUSE...

I AM GRATEFUL FOR MY BACK BECAUSE...

I AM GRATEFUL FOR MY STOMACH BECAUSE...

I AM GRATEFUL FOR MY HIPS BECAUSE...

I AM GRATEFUL FOR MY PELVIC REGION BECAUSE...

I AM GRATEFUL FOR MY THIGHS BECAUSE...

I AM GRATEFUL FOR MY SHINS AND CALVES BECAUSE...

I AM GRATEFUL FOR MY FEET BECAUSE...

Our caregivers model how to give thanks (or the absence of giving it). Did your family/caregivers express thankfulness growing up? If so, what did they express thanks for? How did they express their thanks? Do you presently engage in these same behaviors? What gratitude behaviors would you like to engage in?

_____

_____

_____

_____

_____

_____

_____

_____

_____

_____

_____

_____

_____

A Letter of Thanks

The practice of writing out your gratitude can help you strengthen the wiring of a positive mindset in your brain. In this exercise, you'll identify someone whom you are grateful for and write them a letter of thanks below. Think about all of the aspects of that person you are grateful for. For example, you can acknowledge helpful behaviors they've engaged in and personality traits they hold that you love. When you're finished with the letter, you may choose to actually give it to them. That part is up to you!

_____

_____

_____

_____

_____

_____

Name something positive that has happened to you recently. What made this experience a positive one? Then write down why you are grateful for this experience.

_____

_____

_____

_____

_____

_____

Strengths Garden

Most of us rarely identify and acknowledge our inner strengths and resiliencies. By simply acknowledging them more frequently, we can let our minds blossom with more positivity! That's what this practice is all about. In the area provided, draw a garden with different fauna and flora that represent your strengths. Be intentional in your selections, including the plants and animals you select to represent certain strengths, the colors you use, and any other details you'd like to include. Then answer the questions that follow to reflect on this process.

Reflection questions:

1. **How did it feel to draw your strengths garden?**

    _____

    _____

2. **What impacted your color choices?**

    _____

    _____

3. **Is your garden full and bountiful or sparse and isolated?**

    _____

    _____

4. **Which strength is the largest?**

    _____

    _____

5. **What are the reasons you selected certain flora or fauna to represent specific strengths?**

    _____

    _____

6. **What seeds do you hold to plant future strengths?**

    _____

    _____

Identify people in your life you are grateful for. This can be anyone (alive, passed, someone you personally know, someone you've never met, a mentor, a hero). What are the reasons you're grateful for these people?

SUPPORTIVE TOUCH

Supportive touch is a lovely experience that most of us have never been taught or experienced. It has been found to significantly decrease stress hormones and increase the feel-good hormone oxytocin. So, what is supportive touch? It is the simple act of offering yourself physical comfort by touching your body in kind, gentle ways. It will likely feel unnatural and awkward at first, as this is something new for you! Most of us are not used to showing our bodies unconditional love. Use this practice any time you're in need of comfort or a feel-good boost.

Here are some examples of supportive touch you can try:

→ Place a hand on your chest over your heart and then place your other hand on top of it. Feel the warmth and gentle pressure that this creates.
→ Place one hand on your cheek. Gently cup your cheek in your palm. Notice the sensations that arise in your hand and face.
→ Softly stroke your skin with your fingers. Notice the textures and what shows up in your experience.
→ Cross your arms over your body to hug yourself. Give yourself a soft squeeze.
→ Place one hand on your chest over your heart and one hand on your belly. Feel the movement of these areas as you breathe.

You can also ask trusted loved ones to supportively touch you. Here are some forms of supportive touch you can engage in with another:

→ Embrace in a hug.
→ Rub your back.
→ Hold hands.
→ Gently massage your hands.
→ Lie with your bodies softly pressed together.

Supportive touch is truly a magnificent experience when you let yourself surrender to it. Enjoy!

WHERE DO YOU FEEL APPRECIATION IN YOUR BODY?

The next time you feel truly immersed in gratitude, notice your bodily experience. Notice if you feel warm or full in any areas. Notice any areas of relaxation. Notice what happens to your breath. Does the pace change? Does the depth change? Does where you feel it the most in your body change? Become one with your body in that moment. Let yourself fully feel what is showing up for you. By tuning in to your body in this moment of deep gratitude, you will amplify these feelings, while also allowing yourself to appreciate the experience of appreciation (meta, I know). Additionally, it will help you in the future to attune to smaller moments of appreciation that you may normally ignore, as this insight will allow you to pinpoint the correlation between these bodily sensations and the gratitude you are experiencing.

Maslow's Hierarchy of Needs

If you struggle with finding areas of your life to be grateful for, it can be helpful to take a look at Maslow's Hierarchy of Needs. Psychologist Abraham Maslow developed this hierarchy to express how when a base level of need is met, humans naturally seek to achieve the next level of need. You will use the hierarchy to identify different areas that you can express gratitude in your life. If you haven't yet met some of these levels of need, that's okay! It's unlikely that most people will ever reach complete self-actualization in their lives.

SELF ACTUALIZATION
Meeting your
full potential

ESTEEMS NEEDS
Respect, Recognition,
Strength, Accomplishment

BELONGINGESS & LOVE NEEDS
Intimate relationships, Belonging,
Inclusion Relational Connection

SAFETY NEEDS
Security, Resources, Health, Employment,
Morality, Property, Family Stability

PHYSIOLOGICAL NEEDS
Food, Water, Clothing, Shelter, Sleep,
Air, Warmth, Rest, Reproduction

What physiological needs have been met in your life that you can be thankful for?

_____

_____

What safety needs have been met in your life that you can be thankful for?

_____

_____

What belongingness and love needs have been met in your life that you can be thankful for?

_____

_____

What esteem needs have been met in your life that you can be thankful for?

_____

_____

In what areas of your life, if any, do you feel fulfilled?

_____

_____

Identify something that you're looking forward to in the near future. Why are you looking forward to this event? How do you imagine this event will make you feel? This simple reminder shift will foster positivity.

_____

_____

_____

_____

_____

Fostering Gratitude for Distressing Emotions

This is definitely one of the most challenging exercises you will face. I'm going to ask you to try to foster gratitude and appreciation for distressing emotions. This may sound impossible, but I promise you there is a highly impactful purpose to it.

As mentioned earlier in this workbook, distressing emotions play an evolutionary role in how humans survive. These emotions serve to protect us from danger, but they can become over-activated, which leaves us feeling vulnerable. Consequently, we can start to reject and resist these distressing emotions. We bury them within. However, this leads to further suffering as they are trapped inside and are fighting to be acknowledged.

As the amazing self-compassion expert Dr. Kristin Neff put it: **Suffering = Pain x Resistance**.

This means the more you resist your pain, the more you will intensify your suffering. It is when you can surrender to your emotions without overindulging them that you can move through them. Furthermore, it is when you can offer them gratitude and appreciation that you can manage these distressing emotions with more ease in the long term.

Let's practice:

Identify a recent situation that caused you distress.

_____

_____

What distressing emotion(s) showed up for you during/after this situation?

_____

_____

Did you resist or overindulge these emotions when they showed up?

_____

_____

Did these emotions persist or come back stronger at a later time?

_____

_____

How were these emotions trying to protect you during/after this situation?

_____

_____

Write down a statement of gratitude for these emotions.

(Example: I appreciate that my fear was trying to protect me from conflict with my partner.)

_____

_____

Write down a statement that you can tell yourself the next time you feel distressed in this way.

(Example: Even though I want to turn away from this fear, I will attempt to acknowledge and befriend it.)

_____

_____

What aspects of your life provide you comfort? What makes these aspects comforting to you? When we understand what comforts us, we're better prepared to attract comfort in other areas of our lives.

_____

_____

_____

_____

_____

_____

_____

Self-Love Letter

Use the space below to write yourself a letter that expresses gratitude and appreciation. If possible, try to include some self-love. This letter should be empowering and make you feel good. Meditate to clear your mind right before you start. Once you start writing, don't think too hard about it. Just let it flow out. If it's too challenging to write, consider writing the letter to yourself as a child. What would you want to let them know? What gratitude would you share with them? When you're done with the letter, before you read what you've written, answer the reflections prompts on the next page.

\
\
\
\
\
\
\
\
\
\

_____

_____

_____

_____

_____

_____

Reflections:

1. Before you read it, how did it feel to write this letter?

   _____

   _____

   _____

2. Now read the letter. How did it feel to read this message?

   _____

   _____

   _____

3. Offer yourself gratitude for showing up to this challenging task.

   _____

   _____

Know that you can always come back to this letter in times of need. It will be here for you should there be times when your inner critic shows up, in times when you feel great pain and suffering, and in times when you simply are looking for an extra boost.

Identify three areas where you would like to embrace more gratitude in your life. How can you begin integrating gratitude into these areas?

_____

_____

_____

_____

_____

_____

The G.L.A.D. Technique

Developed by Donald Altman, a licensed counselor and author, the G.L.A.D. technique is a tool to aid you in your positive thinking journey. As you've learned, our brains are fixated on the negative. This acronym will help you embrace more positivity in your daily routine or as needed. I'd recommend practicing this at the end of your day so that you have more experiences to pull from.

G: One **Gratitude** that you are thankful for today.
L: One new thing you **Learned** today.
A: One small **Accomplishment** you achieved today.
D: One moment of **Delight** that touched you today.

Now you try it out:

G: What's one thing you are grateful for today? _____

L: What is one thing you learned today?_____

A: What is one thing you accomplished today?_____

D: What is one thing that brought you delight today?_____

Was this task challenging or easy? Why so?

_____

_____

_____

_____

_____

Either way, honor whatever shows up for you and remember that these tools take practice!

What's one part of your personality that you are grateful for? How does this part of you benefit your life? How does it benefit other people's lives? How can you begin to increase your expression of thankfulness for this part of yourself?

_____

_____

_____

_____

_____

_____

LOVING-KINDNESS MEDITATION

Loving-kindness meditations are meditations that cultivate love and kindness toward others, and even toward yourself! These meditations are drenched in gratitude. Below you will find a script for a loving-kindness meditation to practice. When you practice, make sure you're in a comfortable position, either sitting or lying down. Then follow these steps:

1. Gently close your eyes.

2. Begin to notice the sounds around you—notice even the smallest of sounds.

3. Softly turn your attention to your breath. Notice where you feel it the most in your body.

4. Take three deep breaths in and out.

5. Gently turn your attention to your heart. Notice a soft glow coming from this area. And with this glow, notice the warmth of your heart.

6. Now bring to mind someone who loves you deeply. Imagine this person is standing in front of you. Imagine them sending you love and well wishes. Accept the warmth and kindness this person is offering you.

7. Now offer this person warmth and kindness back. Offer them gratitude. Silently repeat these warm wishes three times: "May you be filled with love and kindness. May you live with ease and happiness. May you know how grateful I am for you." Imagine they accept this gesture wholeheartedly, then let their image fade away.

8. Now imagine you are standing in front of yourself. Begin to send yourself this same love and appreciation that your loved one showed you and that you showed your loved one. Silently repeat these words three times: "May I be filled with love and kindness. May I live with ease and happiness. May I know how grateful I am for myself." Allow yourself to accept this love wholeheartedly. Let the image of yourself fade away.

9. Now imagine a neutral person in your life, someone you aren't close to and to whom you don't have any emotional attachments. Begin sending them this love and appreciation. Silently repeat these words three times: "May you be filled with love and kindness. May you live with ease and happiness. May you know how grateful I am for you." Imagine they accept this gesture wholeheartedly, then let their image fade away.

10. Now imagine all worldly beings in front of you within a small globe. Begin sending them these well wishes. Silently repeat these words three times: "May you be filled with love and kindness. May you live with ease and happiness. May you know how grateful I am for you." Imagine they accept this gesture wholeheartedly, then let their image fade away.

11. Take three deep breaths in and out.

12. Begin to notice the sounds around you. When you are ready, softly open your eyes.

After completing this meditation, check in with how you feel. Take note of what arose for you during this meditation. Identify any judgments or challenges that came up. Also give yourself space to acknowledge any moments of ease and pleasure that you experienced. Remember that the warmth of your heart is always there to offer kindness and gratitude.

Write about an event in your life that you are grateful for. Share specific details about what made this event special to you. Acknowledging the special details will allow you to foster more of them in the future.

_____

_____

_____

_____

_____

_____

_____

GRATITUDE JAR

Gratitude jars are a fun way to embrace thankfulness in your life! All you have to do is find a jar, cut up some pieces of paper, write down anything that makes you feel grateful, and stick the papers in the jar. Or if you're inspired to be more creative, you can decorate your jar, name it something fun, and make your submissions to the jar ornamental. The awesome thing about this jar is that you can keep adding to it over time; you do not have to fill it all at once. Then, when you're feeling down, you can open your jar and read all of your entries to remind yourself of all of the things you have to be thankful for. (Mine is sitting next to me on my desk as I type this book!)

Seven Days of Gratitude

As you've learned, affirmations are a great tool for cultivating new skills because they help shift your mindset! Here you will identify seven different gratitude affirmations that you can embrace during the week. I recommend that each new day you write your affirmation on a sticky note and place it somewhere you will see it throughout your day (e.g., on your bathroom mirror, steering wheel, or computer screen).

Sunday: I am grateful for _____

because _____.

Monday: I am grateful for _____

because _____.

Tuesday: I am grateful for_____

because _____.

Wednesday: I am grateful for _____

because _____.

Thursday: I am grateful for _____

because _____.

Friday: I am grateful for _____

because _____.

Saturday: I am grateful for _____

because _____.

I am filled with gratitude for how far I've come, and I am filled with gratitude for how much further I can go.

Conclusion

Let me end this chapter by saying thank you. I deeply appreciate your commitment to shifting your mindset for your own well-being. Furthermore, in doing so, you're also modeling self-care and how to heal intergenerational trauma for others around you. And speaking of others, how about we start exploring your support squad?

"Acknowledging the good that you already have in your life is the foundation for all abundance."

—Eckhart Tolle

CHAPTER SEVEN

BUILD YOUR SUPPORT SQUAD

As humans, we are innately social creatures. It is in our nature to develop deep connections with others. This aids in survival and makes life a whole lot more entertaining. Our relational connections also play a significant role in our mindset. You can completely change your experience by shifting what kind of people you keep in your life or by asking others to grow with you. It can be a challenge to start to transform these relationships, but, ultimately, it's incredibly rewarding to foster healthier connections. In this chapter, you'll explore the relationships in your life, look at the role of trust, identify different types of relationships, and take tangible steps toward developing a healthy support system.

Many of us learned about how to reach out for support (or not to reach out) from our families while growing up. What were you specifically taught about reaching out for support? Was it considered a strength or a weakness? Consequently, how does it currently feel for you to have to reach out to others in times of need?

_____

_____

_____

_____

_____

_____

_____

_____

_____

_____

_____

_____

Is This a Healthy Relationship?

In this True/False exercise, you'll examine your knowledge of what healthy relationships and boundaries look like. If there's a difference between what you know is the "right answer" and how you feel or act, make a note of that difference. You'll find an answer key underneath the prompts. With the information you gain, you'll be able to begin exploring your current relationships and determine if any changes are needed.

1. **True or False** One person should have more power than the other in the relationship, because there needs to be a clear leader.

2. **True or False** It is not self-centered to place my needs first.

3. **True or False** Couples therapy is only for couples who are on the verge of breaking up.

4. **True or False** It's better to apologize and move on rather than to talk through a situation.

5. **True or False** It's selfish to say no to someone in need.

6. **True or False** Taking space from someone you love is healthy.

7. **True or False** One needs to distance themselves emotionally from others in order to do inner work.

8. **True or False** Low self-worth leads to unhealthy boundaries.

9. **True or False** I shouldn't compromise my core values or beliefs just to make my partner happy.

10. **True or False** If you are in a healthy relationship, you shouldn't have to work very hard at it.

11. **True or False** My partner should automatically know how I'm feeling.

12. **True or False** When growth happens in a relationship, both partners need to be willing to heal and change.

Answer key:
False: 1, 3, 4, 5, 7, 10, 11 • True: 2, 6, 8, 9, 12

How do you typically reach out for support? To whom do you normally go? Do the people you go to for support generally make you feel better or worse? Sometimes our current support systems are not the most helpful. Reflecting on these questions will allow you to determine if you'd benefit from making changes to your support system.

_____

_____

_____

_____

_____

_____

MINDFUL LISTENING

It's so easy to get caught up in our thoughts or distractions like social media instead of being attentive when others are speaking. This exercise will help you practice mindful listening to cultivate deeper connections with your loved ones.

1. Close your eyes and begin to notice what you hear.

2. Listen to the sounds far away. These are the sounds outside of your immediate area.

3. Listen to the sounds immediately in the space around you. Notice all sounds, even the smallest of sounds, such as creaks from the building or the whir of a fan.

4. Turn your attention to the sounds coming from your body. Perhaps you can hear the sound of your breath or your heartbeat.

5. Open your ears to all sounds. Try not to focus on one particular sound but rather imagine your ears are receptive to all sounds at once.

6. When you are ready, open your eyes and reflect on how this experience of mindful listening impacted you.

Trust is an important part of healthy support systems. What does the word *trust* mean to you? What makes someone trustworthy? Do you find it easy or challenging to trust others? Do you find it easy or challenging to trust yourself? Reflecting on trust will allow you to begin to examine your relationships more closely and provide you with insight to create change (as needed).

_____

_____

_____

_____

_____

_____

_____

_____

_____

Filling Up Your Cup

Filling up your own cup means prioritizing your needs. This allows you to replenish your energy and live a healthier lifestyle. Furthermore, doing so allows you to show up in healthier ways for others. Remember, you can't pour from an empty cup. In the space provided, write or draw in the cup different ways you can fill up your own cup. Examples of things you might fill your cup with include self-care, setting boundaries, and positive self-talk.

Boundaries are the limitations you place on relationships that determine the amount of physical and emotional space between you and others. What boundaries do you hold in your relationships? Do you feel comfortable saying no to others? Do you feel comfortable saying yes to others? This knowledge will allow you to begin shifting any boundaries that may be unhealthy. Remember, small steps are totally okay!

_____

_____

_____

_____

_____

_____

Boundary Work

Maintaining healthy boundaries takes balance and practice. Most of us haven't been taught what healthy boundaries look like or seen them modeled for us. Below you will learn about three types of boundaries and their definitions. Then you will practice shifting that information into personal insight!

Rigid boundaries are boundaries in which you emotionally distance/cut yourself off from another (example: refusing to communicate during conflict).

1. Identify one rigid boundary that you engage in.

   _____
   _____

2. How does this boundary aim to protect you?

   _____
   _____

3. What's one step you can take to shift this boundary to make it healthier?

   _____
   _____

Porous boundaries are boundaries in which you're overly emotionally involved with another (example: tolerating someone's hurtful language).

1. Identify one porous boundary that you engage in.

   _____
   _____

2. How does this boundary aim to protect you?

   _____
   _____

3. What's one step you can take to shift this boundary to make it healthier?

   _____
   _____

Healthy boundaries are boundaries in which you appropriately differentiate yourself from another (example: happily helping others when you have the time and energy).

1. Identify one healthy boundary that you engage in.

_____

_____

2. How does this boundary aim to protect you?

_____

_____

3. What's one step you can take to shift this boundary to make it healthier?

_____

_____

Please note: It is totally valid for you to distance yourself from and/or cut off people who are abusive or unwilling to shift your relationship to be healthier.

How we manage toxic interactions and relationships plays an important role in setting healthy boundaries. Some people tend to distance themselves while others may unnecessarily apologize in an attempt to soothe others. How do you typically manage unhealthy situations? Knowing your present responses will allow you to determine if you'd like to change them.

_____

_____

_____

_____

ATTACHMENT STYLES

In her research on infant-caregiver relationships, psychologist Mary Ainsworth found that there are four different attachment styles that humans display in relationships based on their experiences of caregiver attention in early childhood.

First is anxious-preoccupied attachment style, in which one's anxiety fixates on attention from a significant other. People with anxious-preoccupied attachment style tend to be needy and clingy.

Second is fearful-avoidant attachment style, in which one wants to be close to others but has difficulty achieving healthy attachment due to distrust and a fear of rejection. People with fearful-avoidant attachment style tend to be inconsistent and have difficulty regulating their emotions.

Third is dismissive-avoidant attachment style, in which one isolates themselves from others and avoids deep connection. People who are dismissive-avoidant tend to be overly independent and emotionally distant.

Fourth is secure attachment style, in which one maintains equitable relationships that employ healthy boundaries. People with secure attachment style are typically able to explore more of themselves as they have a secure base as a foundation. If you fall outside of secure attachment, don't worry. Thankfully, you can change your attachment style using tools such as the ones in this workbook.

Attachment Style Checklist

Below, check off the statements that resonate with you. The area with the most checkmarks is likely your attachment style. See the sidebar for more details on what each attachment style means. Please note: This is not a formal assessment, but it can guide you in learning more about yourself.

Anxious-Preoccupied

☐ I often latch on to others.

☐ I tend to want other people to like me.

☐ I have detailed fantasies about what a relationship will look like.

☐ When others pull away from me, I tend to act out.

☐ I often feel anxious and worry that someone doesn't like me as much as I like them.

Fearful-Avoidant

☐ I have difficulty trusting others.

☐ When I get too close to someone, I tend to pull away because I'm afraid I'll get hurt.

☐ My relationships tend to look dramatic and unpredictable.

☐ My worst fear is getting rejected.

☐ I feel more anxious as the relationship gets deeper.

Dismissive-Avoidant

☐ I don't like getting involved with others.

☐ I prefer to be independent and self-sufficient.

☐ I tend to be emotionally distant.

☐ It is a bit challenging for me to connect deeply to others.

☐ Relationships are not a priority in my life.

Secure

☐ Intimate relationships are comforting to me.

☐ I feel confident and trusting in my close relationships.

☐ My relationships have healthy reciprocity.

☐ Healthy emotional expression is easy for me in relationships.

☐ I am flexible and communicative in my relationships.

Which attachment style did your responses indicate you engage in?

_____

What, if any, changes in attachment would you like to work toward?

_____

Do you tend to put others before yourself or yourself before others? Identify a few examples of how this shows up in your life. Knowing this information will allow you to determine if you need to make adjustments.

_____

_____

_____

_____

_____

_____

Self-Confidence Scale

This exercise will help you assess your confidence levels. You'll also identify three areas in which you can foster more confidence. Remember, there is a difference between confidence and cockiness. Cockiness is a form of arrogance in which someone has a high opinion of themselves. Confidence is an important aspect of maintaining healthy relationships with others and yourself!

Using the scale below, rate how much you agree with the following statements:

1 = Strongly Disagree
2 = Disagree
3 = Neutral
4 = Agree
5 = Strongly Agree

_____ I have a number of qualities that make me likeable.

_____ I am accomplished and have a lot to feel proud of.

_____ I am able to solve problems that come my way.

_____ Overall, I feel satisfied with myself.

_____ In general, I feel worthy of good things.

_____ I have an enjoyable personality.

_____ I feel good about my appearance.

_____ I feel competent when comparing myself to others.

_____ I am just as valuable as others.

_____ I can handle criticism well.

_____ I am not afraid to make mistakes.

_____ I respect myself.

_____ I am easily able to verbalize my needs.

_____ I am able to accept compliments.

_____ I listen to others' perspectives while also holding to my core values.

Notice the areas where you scored low or high. Low scores (1 or 2) may indicate a lack of confidence, while high scores (4 or 5) may indicate healthy levels of confidence.

Three areas where I can foster more confidence:

1. _____

2. _____

3. _____

What is your definition of a healthy relationship? How do you know when a relationship becomes unhealthy?

_____

_____

_____

_____

_____

SELF-DIFFERENTIATION

Self-differentiation is the balance between independent living and connected relationships. Highly differentiated people are able to find security within and engage in appropriate boundaries with others, while less-differentiated people are either emotionally fused to or emotionally distant from others.

Emotional fusion is personalizing others' emotional situations as our own and projecting our emotions onto others. People who fuse tend to lose themselves in a relationship. Emotional distance is rigidity in becoming close to significant others. People who distance tend to isolate themselves.

High self-differentiation presents as not falling into either of these traps by maintaining healthy independence with continued connection. This is a balancing act. It takes practice, but you can do it!

Trust and Vulnerability

By responding to the prompts below, you'll begin to explore your relationship with trust and vulnerability. Be creative! If you have trouble answering any of these questions, try not to judge yourself. Developing healthy trust and vulnerability takes practice. You can always ask a trusted friend what they would write down about you.

One way I can communicate more effectively:

_____

_____

One affirmation I can use when trying to trust:

_____

_____

One way I can appropriately express my emotions to another:

_____

_____

One thing I can do when I notice a red flag in a relationship:

_____

_____

One way I can show up more honestly in relationships:

_____

_____

One way that someone can earn my trust:

_____

_____

One way I can begin trusting myself more:

_____

_____

One example of a trusting relationship:

_____

_____

One way I can evaluate my present relationships:

_____

_____

One moment I was successfully vulnerable with another:

_____

_____

One way I can take responsibility for my actions:

_____

_____

One way I can maintain healthy differentiation in relationships:

_____

_____

One act that shows me I am respected:

_____

_____

One way to check in with myself when I am feeling unsure:

_____

_____

How do you typically communicate your needs (if at all)? Identify two steps you could take to communicate your needs in a healthier way.

_____

_____

_____

_____

_____

Identifying Different Supports for Different Reasons

Different people in your life will offer different types of support. It's important to be thoughtful in choosing who you go to for different needs. For example, perhaps you go to someone wanting them to just listen to you but instead they immediately offer you advice. In this scenario, you likely won't feel very supported. The prompts below will help you begin to differentiate between different supports you have in your life.

Someone you can go to when you need validation: _____

Someone you can go to when you need a laugh: _____

Someone you can go to when you need a hug: _____

Someone you can go to when you need a distraction: _____

Someone you can go to when you need advice: _____

Someone you can go to when you need someone to just listen: _____

Someone you can go to who will give you a different perspective: _____

What are a couple of areas in your life that you would like more support in? Identify one step you can take toward developing support for each area.

_____

_____

_____

_____

_____

_____

A MINDFUL CONVERSATION

This practice can be used with your significant other, a family member, or a friend. All you need is their buy-in to practice a mindful conversation. Mindful conversations contribute to a positive mindset, as they help us decrease emotional impulsivity, be intentional in our communication, and foster deeper connection. Use the steps below to help guide you in this process.

1. **Schedule a set amount of time to engage in the conversation.**

   Determine how long you want to practice your mindful conversation. I'd suggest starting with smaller amounts of time (15 to 30 minutes) and then moving to longer amounts of time with practice.

2. **Remove any distractions.**

   Turn off your TV and Spotify playlist. Put your phones on silent and put them away. This is a time to be fully present in your conversation, so you don't want anything there tempting you.

3. **Take turns and consider using conversation starters.**

   Make sure you offer equal time for you and your conversation partner to speak. I suggest you google "mindful conversation prompts" if you need support in guiding the conversation.

4. **Think before you speak.**

   Before you talk to your conversation partner, pause for a moment of silence. Consider what you want to say to your partner and the different ways you can say it. Consider what tone you will use to share your message.

5. **Use intentional language.**

   Intentional language is healthy communication that gets your point across in an effective way. Think about how your language and tone may impact your conversation partner. It can be helpful to use "I" statements that reflect your experience. For example, "I feel happy when you tell me that you love me."

6. **Engage in active listening.**

Instead of thinking of the next thing you will say, listen to what your conversation partner is saying to you. Hold appropriate eye contact and use thoughtful body language. Do not interrupt. Once your conversation partner is done speaking, ask clarifying questions if you were unsure about anything that they said.

7. **Reflect what the other person is saying to you.**

Once you feel clear about what the other person said, paraphrase or summarize what your conversation partner said to you. This helps your partner know that you understand what they shared with you, while offering them the chance to correct you if you misunderstood them.

8. **Notice judgments and impulses as they arise.**

Be attentive to any criticisms that may pop up in your mind during the conversation. These may be judgments of yourself, of your partner, or of the content you're speaking about. Furthermore, be thoughtful about any impulses to speak without intention or to react based on emotions.

9. **As you wrap up, offer statements of gratitude.**

Have yourself and your conversation partner offer each other statements of gratitude for showing up for this mindful conversation. After, offer yourself a statement of gratitude for showing up in this new way!

10. **Reflect on how the experience was for you.**

Take a moment to consider how this mindful conversation felt for you. What showed up for you during the conversation? What showed up for you after the conversation? There are no right or wrong answers to this. Simply honor whatever showed up.

Boundary Areas

There are infinite areas of your life where you can hold boundaries. Below you will brainstorm different boundaries you hold in different areas of your life. Then you'll identify if the boundary is rigid, porous, or healthy. The goal of this practice is to help you gain insight into different boundaries so that you may begin to shift any that appear unproductive.

Physical Boundary: a boundary you hold around your physical being (example: not letting others touch your hair).

Do you engage in physical boundaries? YES or NO

One example of a physical boundary you engage in:

_____

Is this boundary RIGID, POROUS, or HEALTHY? _____

Emotional Boundary: a boundary you hold around your emotions (example: holding emotional space for your friends).

Do you engage in emotional boundaries? YES or NO

One example of an emotional boundary you engage in:

_____

Is this boundary RIGID, POROUS, or HEALTHY? _____

Sexual Boundary: a boundary you hold around sexual interactions (e.g., having sex anytime your significant other wants it).

Do you engage in sexual boundaries? YES or NO

One example of a sexual boundary you engage in:

_____

Is this boundary RIGID, POROUS, or HEALTHY? _____

Time Boundary: a boundary you hold around time with others (e.g., not offering your time to help someone move).

Do you engage in time boundaries? YES or NO

One example of a time boundary you engage in:

_____

Is this boundary RIGID, POROUS, or HEALTHY? _____

Intellectual Boundary: a boundary you hold around your intellectual property (example: allowing someone to take your idea and say it was their own).

Do you engage in intellectual boundaries? YES or NO

One example of an intellectual boundary you engage in:

_____

Is this boundary RIGID, POROUS, or HEALTHY? _____

Material Boundary: a boundary you hold around material items (e.g., only letting trusted loved ones borrow money).

Do you engage in material boundaries? YES or NO

One example of a material boundary you engage in:

_____

Is this boundary RIGID, POROUS, or HEALTHY? _____

Energy Boundary: a boundary you hold around your energy (example: limiting how frequently you will listen to a friend's struggles).

Do you engage in energy boundaries? YES or NO

One example of an energy boundary you engage in:

_____

Is this boundary RIGID, POROUS, or HEALTHY? _____

Identify a time that you successfully utilized a support. How did you reach out for support? What did the support do that helped you?

_____

_____

_____

_____

_____

_____

Support Plan

In this exercise, you will develop a personalized support plan to utilize in times of need using the insight that you've acquired throughout this chapter. You can always update your plan as needed!

Signs that I need support:

1. _____

2. _____

3. _____

Coping skills/self-care I can embrace:

1. _____

2. _____

3. _____

Places I can go to not feel isolated:

1. _____

2. _____

3. _____

Friends and/or family I can reach out to:

	Person	Relationship	Phone Number/Email
1.			
2.			
3.			
4.			

Professional support:

Type	Name	Phone Number/Email
Mental Health Professional		
Doctor		
Local Urgent Care		
Emergency		

Reasons it's okay to seek support:

1. _____

2. _____

3. _____

Affirmations I can say before reaching out:

1. _____

2. _____

3. _____

When I am vulnerable, I am brave.

Conclusion

I'm sure this chapter gave you a lot to think about in terms of your relationships and support systems. How are you feeling right now? What are your expectations for taking this information with you in your daily life? Remember, this is a lot of information and it takes time to put into practice. You are truly engaging in this healing journey by simply showing up for yourself in all of these activities! Thankfully, the final chapter will help you navigate taking all of this information forward for long-term success.

"You can't achieve anything entirely by yourself. There's a support system that is a basic requirement of human existence. To be happy and successful on earth, you just have to have people that you rely on."

—**Michael Schur,** *creator of* Parks and Recreation *and* Brooklyn Nine-Nine

CHAPTER EIGHT

THINK POSITIVELY EVERY DAY

Can you believe that you are at the final chapter? You may have some concerns about how you will continue this journey after completing this workbook. Don't worry. This chapter is here to help set you up for long-term success! Here you will integrate what you have learned in previous chapters, identify takeaways, reflect on the shifts you've already made, and strategize to ensure your continued success on your positive mindset journey.

Positive Mindset Assessment

Let's end this journey where you started off: with a positive mindset assessment! Circle the response that best represents your relationship to the statements provided. After you've completed the assessment, compare your responses to those you gave at the beginning of chapter 3.

1. **During my day, I take time to be mindful (present in the moment without judgment).**

    1. Never
    2. Rarely
    3. Sometimes
    4. Usually
    5. Almost Always

2. **I engage in positive self-talk when I need encouragement.**

    1. Never
    2. Rarely
    3. Sometimes
    4. Usually
    5. Almost Always

3. **I show myself self-compassion (understanding and kindness) when I don't meet expectations set by myself or others.**

    1. Never
    2. Rarely
    3. Sometimes
    4. Usually
    5. Almost Always

4. **I recognize my thoughts aren't necessarily fact, and I don't believe everything I think.**

    1. Never
    2. Rarely
    3. Sometimes
    4. Usually
    5. Almost Always

5. **I forgive myself when I make mistakes.**

    1. Never
    2. Rarely
    3. Sometimes
    4. Usually
    5. Almost Always

6. **I communicate my needs to others in healthy ways.**

    1. Never
    2. Rarely
    3. Sometimes
    4. Usually
    5. Almost Always

7. **I try to maintain flexibility in my life, as I understand that life isn't linear.**

    1. Never
    2. Rarely
    3. Sometimes
    4. Usually
    5. Almost Always

8. **I let myself feel my emotions without suppressing or overindulging them.**

    1. Never
    2. Rarely
    3. Sometimes
    4. Usually
    5. Almost Always

9. **I take time to ask myself where my negative thoughts come from.**

    1. Never
    2. Rarely
    3. Sometimes
    4. Usually
    5. Almost Always

10. **I acknowledge and nurture my mind-body-soul connection.**

    1. Never
    2. Rarely
    3. Sometimes
    4. Usually
    5. Almost Always

11. **When looking back at the past, I recall and acknowledge the positive moments I have experienced.**

    1. Never
    2. Rarely
    3. Sometimes
    4. Usually
    5. Almost Always

12. **I have optimism and hope for the future.**

    1. Never
    2. Rarely
    3. Sometimes
    4. Usually
    5. Almost Always

13. **I believe that people (including me) can change.**

    1. Never
    2. Rarely
    3. Sometimes
    4. Usually
    5. Almost Always

Add up the scores from each of your answers using the scale below:

Never = 0 point
Rarely = 1 points
Sometimes = 2 points
Usually = 3 points
Almost Always = 4 points

Q1___ + Q2___ + Q3___ + Q4___ + Q5___ + Q6___ + Q7___ + Q8___ +

Q9___ + Q10___ + Q11___ + Q12___ + Q13___ = Total ___

0 to 25 = Positive Mindset Novice

If you scored in this range, you're likely struggling with prominent negative thinking. Don't let this get you down! By actively using the tools presented in this workbook, you are set up to rewire your brain to embrace positivity!

26 to 36 = Positive Mindset Apprentice

If you scored in this range, you already have some positive mindset tools under your belt! Awesome! You are going to keep building on these skills, and with practice, you'll quickly become a pro.

37 to 52 = Positive Mindset Pro

If you scored in this range, you already engage in some radical positive thinking. Congrats! You're set up to apply these skills in all areas of your life via this workbook!

Reflect on the comparison between today's scores and previous scores:

_____

_____

_____

There is no doubt that you've already seen change since beginning this workbook and diving into the positive mindset journey. Overall, what are some aspects of your life that have shifted or changed? How did this change occur?

_____

_____

_____

_____

_____

_____

_____

_____

Identify three areas of insight that you garnered in this journey. How has gaining this insight impacted your journey?

_____

_____

_____

_____

_____

_____

_____

_____

_____

_____

_____

_____

Scheduling in Self-Care

Throughout this workbook, you've begun to identify and create rituals out of self-care. In this exercise, you'll take these actions a step further by identifying specific scheduling you can utilize for these different self-care activities. Feel free to refer back to chapters 3 and 5 if you need a reminder of the kinds of self-care you have identified.

3 Daily Self-Care Activities:

1. _____

2. _____

3. _____

3 Weekly Self-Care Activities:

1. _____

2. _____

3. _____

3 Monthly Self-Care Activities:

1. _____

2. _____

3. _____

3 Yearly Self-Care Activities:

1. _____

2. _____

3. _____

Next, schedule your daily/weekly self-care activities using the table below:

	Sunday	Monday	Tuesday
4 to 6 a.m.			
6 to 8 a.m.			
8 to 10 a.m.			
10 a.m. to 12 p.m.			
12 to 2 p.m.			
2 to 4 p.m.			
4 to 6 p.m.			
6 to 8 p.m.			
8 to 10 p.m.			
10 p.m. to 12 a.m.			

Wednesday	Thursday	Friday	Saturday

Managing Backdraft and Self-Sabotage

As you move forward in your positive mindset journey, it's helpful to have a plan should backdraft and self-sabotage arise. As a reminder, backdraft is the self-critical patterns and distressing emotions that arise as you begin your healing journey. Self-sabotage is the act of stopping yourself from engaging in healthy behaviors and/or growth. Both backdraft and self-sabotage are functions of your inner critic. Using the prompts below, you'll identify a moment of backdraft or self-sabotage that you've engaged in. This will help you continue to be aware of any setbacks to positive thinking.

Identify the emotion that you felt in that moment:

_____

Identify what thoughts or cognitions you had in that moment:

_____

Identify what physical response you had in that moment:

_____

Validate why this response was showing up by identifying its protective function:

_____

Did you support yourself in that moment? If so, how?

_____

Identify three ways you can support yourself in the future should this backdraft or self-sabotage arise:

1. _____

2. _____

3. _____

Have your relationships and/or communication with others changed since the beginning of this journey? If so, how? Identify any specific boundaries that you have shifted as well.

_____

_____

_____

_____

_____

_____

_____

_____

_____

_____

_____

FIVE TOOLS FOR LONG-TERM SUCCESS

1. **Use a calendar.** Schedule in everything. And I mean everything: work, rest, vacation, play, hobbies, family time, Netflix, etc. This will help you start to balance out different areas of your life and bring more attention to the areas that you tend to ignore.

2. **Practice daily gratitude.** Either in the morning when you wake up or before you go to sleep, take a moment to identify something you are grateful for. As you've learned, gratitude fosters a healthier mindset. This is a really easy and accessible way to slowly rewire your brain toward positivity.

3. **Embrace your support systems.** You can't do everything! We need to rely on others to help us if we want to be successful in the long run. If you have a lot on your plate, ask yourself what responsibilities you can give to someone else. Also, as you determine who your trusted supports are, reach out to them in times of distress. Trusted supports care about you and will want to be there for you.

4. **Be unapologetically authentic.** Don't fall into the trap of rejecting a part of yourself if it doesn't fall into the norm. Embrace your true desires. Also, show up honestly in communication with those around you. Authenticity feeds happiness and long-term alignment with your truest self.

5. **Rest and recharge.** It is productive to rest. Rest restores your energy. If you are depleted of your energy, you cannot accomplish nearly as much. Those who take time to rest are more productive than those who do not. As mentioned above, schedule this time in. You deserve it.

Furthering Your Authentic Narrative

In chapter 5, you began scripting a new, positive self-narrative that embraces your authentic self and comes from a place of empowerment. This exercise asks you to go back and read the narrative you wrote. Then you'll update the narrative by further adding to it. What insights have you learned about your old self-narrative? What has been added to your narrative since chapter 5? You're beginning to cultivate a more well-rounded understanding of yourself in this world.

_____

_____

_____

_____

_____

_____

_____

_____

_____

_____

_____

_____

_____

_____

_____

_____

_____

_____

How has your relationship with yourself shifted since starting this workbook? Have you found that you've been more self-compassionate or able to manage your inner critic with more ease? Furthermore, what changes have you seen in your self-talk?

_____

_____

_____

_____

_____

_____

_____

_____

YOGA NIDRA

Yoga nidra is a meditative practice in which you bring your consciousness into a deep state of relaxation. Unlike the practice of yoga, yoga nidra is not a physical activity and is performed lying down. Use the script below to practice. It can be helpful to have someone else guide you in this practice. You can also use recorded yoga nidra practices by meditation teachers (check out the resources that follow this chapter for some recommendations). Yoga nidra is a truly incredible practice that is supported by research showing that its use can be helpful for those with post-traumatic stress, insomnia, general stress, and anxiety.

1. Lie down (either on a bed, mat, or blanket) with your back toward the earth. Make yourself as comfortable as possible. You can place a pillow under your head or a bolster under your knees if it makes you more comfortable. It's helpful to stay as still as possible during this practice, so make any small adjustments as needed.

2. Gently close your eyes and become present with your breath. Notice the soft movement of your belly move in and out with each breath.

3. Now set an intention for yourself. This may be an affirmation or reason you are engaging in this practice. Say it to yourself in your mind.

4. Next, quickly rotate your consciousness through different areas of your body. As you shift your attention to that area, name the area in your mind. It can also be helpful to imagine a butterfly landing on each spot as you bring your consciousness to it.

   a. Starting with the right side of your body, bring your attention to your right-hand thumb. Index finger. Middle finger. Ring finger. Pinky finger. Palm of the hand. Back of the hand. Wrist. Lower arm. Elbow. Upper arm. Shoulder. Armpit. Side of the body. Hip. Thigh. Knee. Shin. Ankle. Bottom of the foot. Top of the foot. Big toe. Second toe. Third toe. Fourth toe. Fifth toe.

   b. Next, gently bring your attention to the left side of your body, starting with your left-hand thumb. Index finger. Middle finger. Ring finger. Pinky finger. Palm of the hand. Back of the hand. Wrist. Lower arm. Elbow. Upper arm. Shoulder. Armpit. Side of the body. Hip. Thigh. Knee. Shin. Ankle. Bottom of the foot. Top of the foot. Big toe. Second toe. Third toe. Fourth toe. Fifth toe.

c. Moving to the back of your body, bring your attention to the back of your heels. Back of your calves. Back of your knees. Back of your thighs. Buttocks. Lower back. Middle back. Upper back. Neck. Back of the head. Top of the head. Forehead. Eyebrows. Eyes. Temples. Ears. Nose. Cheeks. Lips. Teeth. Tongue. Jawline. Chin. Front of the neck. Collarbone. Chest. Upper abdomen. Middle abdomen. Lower abdomen. Pelvic floor.

d. Now bring your attention to every part of your right side of the body. Left side of the body. Your whole body.

5. Return your awareness to your breath. With each inhale and exhale you will count down from 10. Inhale 10, exhale 10. Inhale 9, exhale 9. Inhale 8, exhale 8. Inhale 7, exhale 7. Inhale 6, exhale 6. Inhale 5, exhale 5. Inhale 4, exhale 4. Inhale 3, exhale 3, Inhale 2, exhale 2. Inhale 1, exhale 1.

6. Feel the weight of your body as if it were getting light and slowly coming off the ground. Sit with this experience. Then feel the weight of your body being pulled down by gravity. Feel your body getting heavier and melt toward the earth.

7. Bring your attention to the space in front of your closed eyelids. Notice the colors, lights, and patterns that you see.

8. Next, you will visualize different scenes. Quickly imagine each before jumping to the next one.

a. Start with a field of orange flowers.

b. A tree blowing in the wind.

c. A cat stretching.

d. An ice cube melting.

e. A close friend laughing.

f. The ocean waves.

g. A pack of puppies playing.

h. A snowy mountain.

i. A warm hug from a loved one.

j. A cozy fire.

9. Now, repeat the intention that you stated in step 3 of this practice. Say it to yourself three times.

10. Softly wiggle your fingers and toes as you start to come out of this practice. As you come into your body, you may gently open your eyes. Come into the room around you.

11. The practice is now complete.

It's only human that we fall back into old patterns at times. It's extremely likely that you'll be confronted with this situation. What can you do when you become aware of these old patterns showing up? How can you encourage yourself should you find this is happening to you?

_____

_____

_____

_____

_____

_____

Play and Pleasure

Let's identify some of the fun things you can continue to integrate into your positive mindset adventure. Do you tend to think of play as something that children do? Well, play is healthy for people of any age! Some examples of play and pleasure include playing board or video games, tickling your significant other, being a member of a recreational sports team, coloring, playing music, dancing, singing, and going on outdoor adventures.

Write down your favorite play activities below:

_____

_____

_____

Write down one type of play you already engage in:

_____

_____

What about this activity gives you pleasure?

_____

_____

How often do you engage in this activity?

_____

_____

How can you continue or increase this playful activity?

_____

_____

Write down another type of play you already engage in:

_____

_____

What about this activity gives you pleasure?

_____

_____

How often do you engage in this activity?

_____

_____

How can you continue or increase this playful activity?

_____

_____

Write down one type of play you don't engage in but would like to:

_____

_____

How may this activity give you pleasure?

_____

_____

What's one step you can take to embrace this play?

_____

_____

When can you schedule this playful activity?

_____

_____

Consider what authentic parts of yourself you've begun to embrace and what insights you've gained over the course of the last few chapters. How has your self-narrative shifted over the course of this workbook? What perceptions about yourself have you let go of and/or embraced?

_____

_____

_____

Sanctuary Imagery

In this visualization exercise, you will imagine a sanctuary space and fully immerse your senses in this imagined safe space. Then you'll put into writing your visualization to solidify and reinforce this positive imagery. The purpose of this imagery is to help you feel calm and peaceful in times of need. Know that you can access this sanctuary space anytime you need it.

Close your eyes and take three deep breaths in and out. Bring your attention to the space in the center of your head. Begin to imagine a space that makes you feel safe. It can be a place that physically exists in this world, or it can be a place that you've imagined. This is a place where you do not have to worry about any harm—a secure place in which you are protected fully. Imagine it as fully as possible.

Once you've fully immersed yourself in this imagery and let yourself sit with the feelings that came up, gently let go of the imagery. Take three deep breaths and open your eyes. Then write down what you imagined.

1. What does this space look like? What colors are present? What textures are present?

   _____

2. Are there any objects present? Are there any other people in this space?

   _____

3. What sounds, if any, are present in this safe space?

   _____

4. What smells, if any, are present in this safe space?

   _____

5. What tastes, if any, are present in this safe space?

   _____

6. What emotions arise as you sit in this space in your mind?

   _____

How can you hold yourself accountable to long-term change without being self-critical?

_____

_____

_____

_____

_____

Honoring Your Accomplishments

Acknowledging your accomplishments and successes is a great motivator and a lovely way to recognize how resilient you have been in your life. Below, you will identify different accomplishments you have achieved in the past, are presently achieving, and are planning on achieving in the future.

Past Accomplishments:

1. _____

2. _____

3. _____

Present Accomplishments:

1. _____

2. _____

3. _____

Future Accomplishments:

1. _____

2. _____

3. _____

Overall, what are your main takeaways from this workbook experience? What challenges have you overcome during this journey?

_____

_____

_____

Alignment Scale

Alignment is about being attuned to your mind, body, and soul. You're fostering alignment on this positive thinking journey! Use the scale below to assess how aligned you presently feel in your life.

Rate the agreeableness of the following statements:

1 = Strongly Disagree
2 = Disagree
3 = Neutral
4 = Agree
5 = Strongly Agree

_____ I feel that I am in a good place in my career, or at least I feel that I am on the right track.

_____ Overall, my mental health feels stable.

_____ I embrace my authentic interests and desires.

_____ I engage in activities that make me feel good about myself.

_____ Others I keep in my life make me feel worthy.

_____ I tend to be open and receptive to growth and healing.

_____ My body receives appropriate attention and care.

_____ I feel independent and highly differentiated from others.

_____ It's easy for me to embrace my creative side.

_____ I believe I am living my life's purpose.

_____ I rarely feel significantly fatigued or drained.

_____ My soul feels acknowledged and full.

When reviewing your responses, note any low scores (1 or 2) and high scores (4 or 5). Low scores may indicate that you're not feeling aligned in your life. High scores may indicate you're feeling very aligned in your life. Use this information to identify three areas where you'd like to increase alignment.

Three areas where I can foster more alignment:

1. _____

2. _____

3. _____

PROGRESSIVE MUSCLE RELAXATION

Progressive muscle relaxation is a practice in which you systematically tense and release the muscles in your body. This is a helpful tool to release stress and shift your mindset. Follow the script below to practice.

1. Lie down and gently close your eyes.

2. Take three deep breaths in and out.

3. On your next inhale, gently squeeze all the muscles in your right leg and foot. Hold your inhale for about 5 seconds. As you exhale, relax all the muscles in your right leg and foot. Notice the flood of energy release and how your muscles relax.

4. Next, take another deep breath and gently squeeze all the muscles in your left leg and foot. Hold your inhale for about 5 seconds. As you exhale, relax all the muscles in your left leg and foot. Notice the flood of energy release and how your muscles relax.

5. Then practice this same breath and muscle engagement with your right arm. And then your left arm.

6. Next, use this same practice with the front side of your torso. Then practice it with your back.

7. Now, with your inhale, gently squeeze your face. Hold for 5 seconds, and with your exhale, release your facial muscles.

8. Finally, engage your breath and your entire body's muscles for 5 seconds. Then release.

9. Notice how your body feels after this practice. When you are ready, open your eyes.

How has completing this workbook taken you closer to achieving your long-term goals and dreams?

_____

_____

_____

_____

_____

_____

_____

10 AFFIRMATIONS FOR RESILIENCE

1. I have already overcome unimaginable setbacks.

2. I am able to adapt to unexpected challenges.

3. I am deserving of good things.

4. Self-compassion is the key to motivation.

5. I am grateful for how far I've come.

6. There are an infinite number of positive possibilities.

7. When I am myself, I am attracting true happiness.

8. Every day I am trying my best and growing beyond my conscious awareness.

9. I am worthy of my own kindness and love.

10. I believe that I will achieve my aligned path and life's purpose.

Offer yourself some words of gratitude for showing up for yourself on this journey!

_____

_____

_____

_____

_____

Planning for the Future

Here you will envision the steps it will take for you to achieve your goals and dreams. It's helpful to break down your long-term vision and goals into smaller, more tangible steps. Below, you'll identify one long-term goal for different life areas, break those long-term goals into short-term goals, and then cultivate small steps you can take in your immediate future to move you toward achieving this goal. Furthermore, you'll identify a support person to aid you on this journey. An example is provided to help guide you.

I encourage you to develop further goals in these areas or in additional areas as you'd like. Some goal areas can include your home, romantic relationships, friendships, family, career, hobbies, travel, physical health, mental health, community, and advocacy. Remember that this isn't about perfection and that flexibility is needed in achieving our long-term goals.

Example:

Home Goal

→ One long-term goal

1. Renovate my kitchen

→ Three short-term goals

1. Come up with ideal design

2. Figure out price range

3. Save money needed to renovate

→ Small steps for immediate action

1. Figure out my budget

2. Make a Pinterest board of inspirational kitchen designs

3. Put $50 aside per week

Now, it's your turn!

Home Goal

→ One long-term goal

1. _____

→ Three short-term goals

1. _____

2. _____

3. _____

→ Small steps for immediate action

1. _____

2. _____

3. _____

→ One support person who can help

1. _____

Relationship Goal (romantic or platonic)

→ One long-term goal

    1. _____

→ Three short-term goals

    1. _____

    2. _____

    3. _____

→ Small steps for immediate action

    1. _____

    2. _____

    3. _____

→ One support person who can help

    1. _____

Family Goal

→ One long-term goal

    1. _____

→ Three short-term goals

    1. _____

    2. _____

    3. _____

→ Small steps for immediate action

    1. _____

    2. _____

    3. _____

→ One support person who can help

    1. _____

Career Goal

→ One long-term goal

    1. _____

→ Three short-term goals

    1. _____

    2. _____

    3. _____

→ Small steps for immediate action

    1. _____

    2. _____

    3. _____

→ One support person who can help

    1. _____

Hobby Goal

→ One long-term goal

    1. _____

→ Three short-term goals

    1. _____

    2. _____

    3. _____

→ Small steps for immediate action

    1. _____

    2. _____

    3. _____

→ One support person who can help

    1. _____

Health Goal

→ One long-term goal

    1. _____

→ Three short-term goals

    1. _____

    2. _____

    3. _____

→ Small steps for immediate action

    1. _____

    2. _____

    3. _____

→ One support person who can help

    1. _____

Look at you, setting yourself up for success!

I am able to overcome what feels hopeless and achieve what may seem impossible.

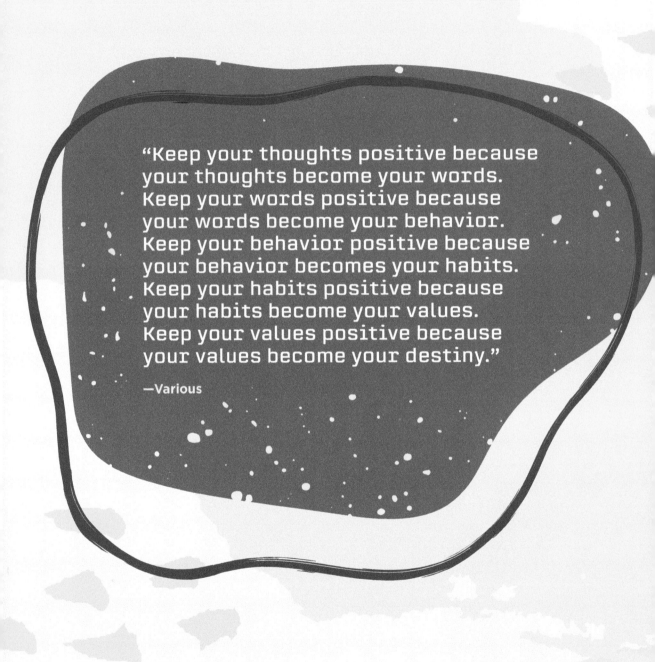

"Keep your thoughts positive because your thoughts become your words. Keep your words positive because your words become your behavior. Keep your behavior positive because your behavior becomes your habits. Keep your habits positive because your habits become your values. Keep your values positive because your values become your destiny."

—Various

Conclusion

I am so proud of you for making it here. You have shown up for yourself in huge ways. Take a moment to honor your journey. You have likely already seen improvements and growth toward a positive mindset, but significant growth and healing are blossoming within you and will become even more apparent with time. Keep using these tools. Keep acknowledging how worthy you are of this journey. I believe in you!

A Final Word on Positive Thinking

Congratulations, my friend! You just accomplished something profound. You invested in your well-being by taking the plunge into this workbook and you did it! Self-work isn't easy, and yet you strapped in and made it to the end. That's no small feat. Hopefully, you're feeling some self-gratitude and letting this journey really sink in. Try not to let any feelings of happiness or pride slip past you in this moment. Let yourself fully feel these emotions. Know you are so worthy of experiencing all these heartwarming feelings. It's also okay if you don't have any positive feelings right now. Honor your journey and know that there is no right or wrong way to experience it. Place a hand over your heart and accept this gentle gesture of gratitude.

I'm truly honored to have guided you through this workbook. It fills my heart with joy to think that you invested in your mental well-being. I know how hard it is to change. I know the strength and resilience that are needed to use these tools. I'm so proud of you. You are so worthy of every moment of self-kindness, self-compassion, and self-care.

I challenge you to continue this journey with just as much vigor. Just because this workbook is ending, it does not mean that your positive mindset journey has to end. You've already changed your life by simply starting this journey. The insights and tools you gathered in this book have equipped you to have a sustainable positive thinking practice. Don't give up on yourself! Know that it's totally normal to have moments of slipping back into old patterns. In fact, you now have the tools to move forward more efficiently than before. Remember, this all takes practice and becomes easier with time.

I have no doubt that you will continue to see the lifelong benefits of what positive thinking has to offer. You will see it fill your life with all kinds of warmth, happiness, and success. It will help you get through the hard times while also helping you savor the good times. Positive thinking is always here for you.

Sending you so much love and joy on your continued journey.

♡ Alexa

Resources

Books

Self-Compassion: The Proven Power of Being Kind to Yourself by Kristin Neff, PhD

The Miracle of Mindfulness: An Introduction to the Practice of Meditation by Thich Nhat Hanh

Mindsight: The New Science of Personal Transformation by Daniel J. Siegel

Braving the Wilderness: The Quest for True Belonging and the Courage to Stand Alone by Brené Brown

There is Nothing Wrong with You: Going Beyond Self-Hate by Cheri Huber

Radical Compassion: Learning to Love Yourself and Your World with the Practice of RAIN by Tara Brach

When Things Fall Apart: Heart Advice for Difficult Times by Pema Chödrön

Hold Me Tight: Seven Conversations for a Lifetime of Love by Dr. Sue Johnson

A New Earth: Awakening to Your Life's Purpose by Eckhart Tolle

No Mud, No Lotus: The Art of Transforming Suffering by Thich Nhat Hanh

Websites

Mindful.org

Self-Compassion.org

CenterForMSC.org

UCLAHealth.org/marc/mindful-meditations

PositivePsychology.com

Therapist Databases

InclusiveTherapists.com

WeGlimmer.com

PsychologyToday.com

References

Ackerman, Courtney. "Cognitive Distortions: When Your Brain Lies to You (+ PDF Worksheets)." PositivePsychology.com, October 31, 2020. https://positivepsychology.com/cognitive-distortions/.

Ackerman, Courtney. "What Is Positive Mindset: 89 Ways to Achieve a Positive Mental Attitude." PositivePsychology.com, October 13, 2020. https://positivepsychology.com/positive-mindset/.

Altman, Donald. *The Mindfulness Toolbox: 50 Practical Mindfulness Tips, Tools, and Handouts for Anxiety, Depression, Stress and Pain.* Eau Claire, WI: PESI Publishing and Media, Incorporated, 2014.

APA Staff. "Trauma." American Psychological Association. American Psychological Association, 2020. https://www.apa.org/topics/trauma.

Attachment Project Staff. "Attachment Styles & Their Role in Relationships." Attachment Project, July 2, 2020. https://www.attachmentproject.com/blog/four-attachment-styles/.

Bergland, Christopher. "Diaphragmatic Breathing Exercises and Your Vagus Nerve." Psychology Today. May 16, 2017. https://www.psychologytoday.com/us/blog/the-athletes-way/201705/diaphragmatic-breathing-exercises-and-your-vagus-nerve.

Bergland, Christopher. "Optimism Stabilizes Cortisol Levels and Lowers Stress." Psychology Today. July 24, 2013. https://www.psychologytoday.com/us/blog/the-athletes-way/201307/optimism-stabilizes-cortisol-levels-and-lowers-stress.

Bloom, Linda. "You've Got the Magic Touch." Psychology Today. January 15, 2018. https://www.psychologytoday.com/us/blog/stronger-the-broken-places/201801/youve-got-the-magic-touch.

Brach, Tara. *Radical Compassion: Learning to Love Yourself and Your World with the Practice of RAIN.* London: Penguin Life, 2019.

Brown, Brené. *Daring Greatly: How the Courage to Be Vulnerable Transforms the Way We Live, Love, Parent, and Lead.* New York, NY: Avery, 2015.

Buchalter, Susan I. *250 Brief, Creative & Practical Art Therapy Techniques: A Guide for Clinicians & Clients.* Eau Claire, WI: PESI Publishing & Media, 2017.

Cherry, Kendra. "Benefits of Positive Thinking for Body and Mind." Verywell Mind, June 1, 2020. https://www.verywellmind.com/benefits-of-positive-thinking-2794767.

Chödrön, Pema. *Start Where You Are: A Guide to Compassionate Living.* Boulder, CO: Shambhala, 2018.

Churchill, Winston. *My Early Life: 1874–1904.* New York, NY: Scribner, 2013.

Craig, Heather. "10 Ways To Build Trust in a Relationship." PositivePsychology.com, October 31, 2020. https://positivepsychology.com/build-trust/.

Cullen, Margaret. "How to Regulate Your Emotions Without Suppressing Them." Greater Good, January 30, 2020. https://greatergood.berkeley.edu/article/item /how_to_regulate_your_emotions_without_suppressing_them.

Datta, K., M. Tripathi, and H. N. Mallick. "Yoga Nidra: An Innovative Approach for Management of Chronic Insomnia—A Case Report." *Sleep Science and Practice* 5, no. 7 (2017). https://doi.org/10.1186/s41606-017-0009-4.

Dawson-Cook, Susan. "Follow This Yoga Nidra Script to Relax." U.S. Masters Swimming, April 1, 2020. https://www.usms.org/fitness-and-training/articles-and-videos /articles/follow-this-yoga-nidra-script-to-relax.

DialecticalBehaviorTherapy.com Staff. "Recognizing Your Emotions." DBT, July 25, 2020. https://dialecticalbehaviortherapy.com/emotion-regulation/recognizing -your-emotions/.

Ferreira-Vorkapic, Camila, et al. "The Impact of Yoga Nidra and Seated Meditation on the Mental Health of College Professors." *International Journal of Yoga* 11, no. 3 (2018): 215–223. doi:10.4103/ijoy.IJOY_57_17.

Fogel, Alan. "Slow Movement with Awareness: Better Than Exercise?" Psychology Today. July 6, 2010. https://www.psychologytoday.com/us/blog/body-sense/201007 /slow-movement-awareness-better-exercise.

Fraley, R. Chris. "A Brief Overview of Adult Attachment Theory and Research Fraley." A Brief Overview of Adult Attachment Theory and Research, 2018. http://labs .psychology.illinois.edu/~rcfraley/attachment.htm.

Gilbert, Roberta M. *Extraordinary Relationships: A New Way of Thinking about Human Interactions.* Stephens City, VA: Leading Systems Press, 2017.

Gold, Taro. *Open Your Mind, Open Your Life: A Book of Eastern Wisdom.* Kansas City, MO: Andrews McMeel Pub., 2002.

Greater Good Staff. "Loving-Kindness Meditation." Greater Good in Action, 2020. https://ggia.berkeley.edu/practice/loving_kindness_meditation.

Hall, T. M., H. G. Kaduson, and C. E. Schaefer. (2001), Fifteen Effective Play Therapy Techniques. *Professional Psychology: Research and Practice,* 33(6), 515–522.

Hạnh, Thich Nhất. *The Heart of the Buddha's Teaching: Transforming Suffering into Peace, Joy & Liberation.* New York, NY: Harmony Books, 2015.

Hanson, Rick. "Confronting the Negativity Bias." Dr. Rick Hanson, August 27, 2019. https://www.rickhanson.net/how-your-brain-makes-you-easily-intimidated/.

Harvard Health Staff. "Giving Thanks Can Make You Happier." Harvard Health, 2020. https://www.health.harvard.edu/healthbeat/giving-thanks-can-make-you-happier.

Homma, Ikuo, and Yuri Masaoka. "Breathing Rhythms and Emotions." *Experimental Physiology* 93, no. 9 (August 14, 2008): 1011–21. https://doi.org/10.1113/expphysiol.2008.042424.

Johns Hopkins Staff. "Diaphragmatic Breathing." Johns Hopkins All Children's Hospital, 2020. https://www.hopkinsallchildrens.org/Services/Anesthesiology/Pain-Management/Complementary-Pain-Therapies/Diaphragmatic-Breathing.

Lee, Louise. "Focus on Small Steps First, Then Shift to the Larger Goal." Stanford Graduate School of Business, May 17, 2017. https://www.gsb.stanford.edu/insights/focus-small-steps-first-then-shift-larger-goal.

Maslow, A. H. "A Theory of Human Motivation." *Psychological Review* 50, no. 4 (1943): 370–96. https://doi.org/10.1037/h0054346.

Mayo Clinic Staff. "Positive Thinking: Stop Negative Self-Talk to Reduce Stress." Mayo Foundation for Medical Education and Research, January 21, 2020. https://www.mayoclinic.org/healthy-lifestyle/stress-management/in-depth/positive-thinking/art-20043950.

Mayo Clinic Staff. "Stress Symptoms: Effects on Your Body and Behavior." Mayo Foundation for Medical Education and Research, April 4, 2019. https://www.mayoclinic.org/healthy-lifestyle/stress-management/in-depth/stress-symptoms/art-20050987.

MHA National Staff. "Person-Centered Language." Mental Health America, 2020. https://www.mhanational.org/person-centered-language.

Murray, Katy. "Container." *Journal of EMDR Practice and Research* 5, no. 1 (2011): 29–32. https://doi.org/10.1891/1933-3196.5.1.29.

Neff, Kristin. "Exercise 4: Supportive Touch." Self-Compassion, June 3, 2019. https://self-compassion.org/exercise-4-supportive-touch/.

Neff, Kristin. *Self-Compassion: The Proven Power of Being Kind to Yourself*. New York, NY: William Morrow, 2015.

Palumbo, Stephanie. "An Interview with Michael Schur." *The Believer*, October 1, 2015. https://believermag.com/an-interview-with-michael-schur/.

Peterson, Laura A. "Decrease Stress by Using Your Breath." Mayo Foundation for Medical Education and Research, March 23, 2017. https://www.mayoclinic.org/healthy-lifestyle/stress-management/in-depth/decrease-stress-by-using-your-breath/art-20267197.

Rogers, Carl R., and Peter D. Kramer. *On Becoming a Person: A Therapist's View on Psychotherapy*. Boston, MA: Houghton Mifflin, 1995.

Saakvitne, Karen W., and Laurie Anne Pearlman. *Transforming the Pain: A Workbook on Vicarious Traumatization*. New York, NY: W. W. Norton & Company, 1996.

Salzberg, Sharon. *Real Love: The Art of Mindful Connection*. New York, NY: Flatiron Books, 2018.

Schuldt, Woody LMHC. "Grounding Techniques (Article)." Therapist Aid, September 22, 2020. https://www.therapistaid.com/therapy-article/grounding-techniques-article.

Siegel, Daniel J. *Mindsight: The New Science of Personal Transformation*. New York, NY: Bantam Books, 2011.

Smookler, Elaine. "How to Practice Mindful Listening." Mindful, April 24, 2019. https://www.mindful.org/how-to-practice-mindful-listening/.

Therapist Aid Staff. "Social Support." Therapist Aid, 2018. https://www.therapistaid.com/worksheets/social-support.pdf.

Tolle, Eckhart. *A New Earth: Awakening to Your Life's Purpose*. London: Penguin Books, 2018.

Index

A

Abundance mindset, 95
Acceptance
  and mindfulness, 36
  radical, 37
  self-, 45–46
Accomplishments, acknowledging, 174
Adaptivity, 80–83
Affirmations
  motivational, 52
  for resilience, 178
Ainsworth, Mary, 138
Alignment, 176
Altman, Donald, 123
Attachment styles, 138–140
Awareness
  body, 21–22
  of feelings and emotions, 16
  mindfulness, 19–20
  present moment, 84
  of thoughts, 17

B

Backdraft, 10–11, 69, 162
Body appreciation, 107, 115
Body scans, 21–22, 43–44
Boundaries, 135–137, 148–149
Brach, Tara, 60
Breathing and breathwork
  about, 21
  belly breathing, 99–100
  mindful breath, 38–39
  through distress, 67
Brown, Brené, x

C

Chödrön, Pema, 54
Churchill, Winston, 2
Cognitions, 4
Cognitive distortions, 94
Communication
  mindful conversation, 146–147
  mindful listening, 132–133

Container exercises, 96–97
Cortisol, 9

D

Dyer, Wayne W., 14

E

Emotional fusion, 142
Emotions. *See* Feelings
    and emotions

F

Feelings and emotions
  balancing, 16
  gratitude for distressing, 118–119
  primary vs. secondary, 62
  sitting with, 40–42
Fight-or-flight response, 6
Filling up your own cup, 134
Flexibility, 80–83, 85
Future planning, 180–182

G

G.L.A.D. technique, 123–124
Gratitude
  assessment, 105–106
  body, 107
  for distressing emotions, 118–119
  jars, 126
  models of, 108
  for others, 113
  as a practice, 103–104
  seven days of, 127
  writing about, 109–110,
      124, 126, 179
Grief, 11
Grounding
  5-4-3-2-1, 57
  techniques, 47
Guided imagery
  about, 20
  observing thoughts, 76–77
  sanctuary imagery, 172

H

Hanh, Thich Nhat, 28
Health benefits, of positive thinking, 9

I

Inner child, letter to, 74–75
Inner critic. *See also* Backdraft
  befriending, 55–56
  externalizing, 65–66
  symptom checklist, 68

J

Journaling, 22

L

Letters
  gratitude, 109–110
  to inner child, 74–75
  self-love, 120–122
Listening, 132–133
Loving-kindness meditation, 124–125

M

Manifestation drawing, 101
Maslow's Hierarchy of Needs, 116–117
McDonald, Michele, 60
Meditation
  about, 20
  loving-kindness, 124–125
  thought observation imagery, 76–77
Meta-judgment, 10
Mindfulness
  about, 19–20
  in conversation, 146–147
  Five A's of, 36–37
  five senses checklist, 50–51
  in language, 87
  in listening, 132–133
  in movement, 87–88
Motivation, 52
Movement, 22, 87–88, 167–169

N

Narratives
  about, 4
  authentic, 165–166

life, 91
  reconstructing trauma, 59
  shifting to positive life, 98–99
Needs, 116–117, 134, 144
Neff, Kristin, 10, 102, 118
Negative bias trap, 7
Negative thinking, 6, 17
"No," saying, 87

O

On Becoming a Person (Rogers), 37

P

Parentification, 75
Perceptions, 4
Physical activity, 22
Play, 170–171
Positive mindset,
    30–33, 154–157
Positive thinking
  benefits of, 8–10
  challenges to, 10–11
  defined, 4–5
  hacks, 19
  and relationships, 7, 9
  self-assessment, 8, 23
  vs. toxic positivity, 5
Progressive muscle
    relaxation, 177

R

Radical acceptance, 37
RAIN technique, 60
Reframing, self-compassionate, 62–64
Relationships. *See also*
    Support networks
  attachment styles, 138–140
  boundaries in, 135–137,
    148–149
  healthy, 131, 142
  positive thinking and, 7, 9
Resilience, 4, 17, 79, 95, 178
Rigidity, 85, 89–90
Rogers, Carl, 37

S

Salzberg, Sharon, 78
Scarcity mindset, 95
Schur, Michael, 152
Self-acceptance, 45–46
Self-care, 34–35, 92–93, 159–161
Self-compassionate reframing, 62–64
Self-confidence, 141–142
Self-differentiation, 142
Self-judgment, 10
Self-love, 120–122
Self-perceptions, 70–73
Self-sabotage, 162
Self-talk, 4, 86–87
Senses
    5-4-3-2-1 grounding, 57
    mindfulness checklist, 50–51
Setbacks, identifying, 48–49
Shame, 6, 58–59
Strengths, 111–112
Stress management, 9
Success tools, 164
Supportive touch, 114
Support networks, 130, 132, 145.
        See also Relationships
Support plans, 150–151

T

Thoughts
    awareness of, 17
    cognitions, 4
    distorted, 94
    negative, 6–7, 17
    observing, 76–77
    sitting with, 18, 40–42
    thought logs, 62–64
Tolle, Eckhart, 128
Toxic positivity, 5
Trauma, 58–59
Trust, 133, 143–144

V

Visualization
    about, 20
    creative, 53
    sanctuary imagery, 172
Vulnerability, 143–144

W

Worthiness, 58

Y

"Yes," saying, 87
Yoga nidra, 167–169

Acknowledgments

Josh, you show up for me at every moment. You ground me when I need it the most, and you offer me unconditional acceptance. I seriously wouldn't be where I am in my mental health journey without you. I wouldn't have written this book without you. Truly, what a dream.

Thanks to my editor, Jed Bickman, for making me feel comfortable and competent during the process of writing my first book. Also, a huge thanks to all of the incredible womxn who have uplifted and empowered me in my life! This includes, but certainly isn't limited to, the therapists who helped me at my lowest; the intersectional feminists who taught me about authenticity and unlearning; my grad school mentor, Dr. Bethany Simmons, who believed in my intellect; and my mom, auntie, and gma who all modeled deep compassion and fierce resilience across my life.

My gratitude overflows for you all.

About the Author

Alexa Brand, MS, LMFT, (she/her) is a psychotherapist and mindfulness mentor who specializes in mindful self-compassion and intersectional approaches to mental health. In 2020, she founded Soul Compassion (SoulCompassion.com), where she provides mindfulness mentorship to clients who are seeking to unlearn toxic norms and embrace their authentic alignment. Alexa also teaches graduate-level psychology courses for student therapists. Alexa is a cis, bisexual womxn who currently resides in Los Angeles, CA, with her spouse, her dog Lemon, and her two cats, Strudel and Dill. Find Alexa on Instagram @MindfulFemme.

CPSIA information can be obtained
at www.ICGtesting.com
Printed in the USA
BVHW051915250421
605801BV00003B/4

9 781648 768279